Signature Tastes
of
SOUTH CAROLINA

SMOKE ALARM

MEDIA

To Stanley Siler and Judy King...for supporting a Georgia-born boy in finding his heart in that foreign country of South Carolina

And oddly enough, to Pat Conroy...beginning with The Boo, your singular affair with the Low-country created the outline of a place that haunts me almost every moment I am away.

To others unnamed, because my memory is as short as my hair.

Welcome to South Carolina: The Palmetto State information and photography from the South Carolina State Museum and Stacey Breitberg

You can find us at www.signaturetastes.com and on Facebook: Signature Tastes of South Carolina.

Layout by Steven W. Siler

Photography by Rosalie Anne Fradella and Steven W. Siler except where noted.

Library of Congress Control Number: 2010914315

Siler, Steven W.

   Signature Tastes of South Carolina: Favorite Recipes from our Local Restaurants

   ISBN 978-1506022581

   1. Restaurants-South Carolina-Guidebooks. 2. Cookery-South Carolina

Printed in the United States of America

This book is dedicated to the emergency responders...

From the first frantic call to 9-1-1
To the comforting hands at Roper
You give your time...

away from spouses,
away from friends,
away from children,
And yes, even from meals...

To assure all of us:

"Tonight, I will make it better for you
no matter what,
I will watch over you..."

I have always wondered if anyone really reads the Table of Contents. Now since this is a cookbook, I should have organized everything under its proper heading, like soups, pasta, desserts and the like. This is not just a cookbook as much as a Culinary Postcard; a celebration of the city itself...about the eateries, fine dining, casual dining, bars, drive -ins, and of course, the people.

TABLE OF CONTENTS

5

> *"...The Inhabitants of Carolina, thro' the Richness of the Soil, live an easy and pleasant Life..."*

John Lawson, British explorer and author

Welcome to South Carolina! This Southeastern state, sandwiched between North Carolina and Georgia, is only the 40th largest in the country, but its many appealing features mean that plenty of people are happy to call it home. With an Atlantic coastline, coastal plains, the unusual carolina bays, expansive reforested areas, the Table Rock State Park, several large lakes, a river popular with whitewater rafters, and even some mountains, its geography is as varied as its culture and history.

Originally, the area was home to many Native American tribes, the largest of which were the Cherokees and Catawbas. In the 16th century, explorers from Spain and France arrived in the area, and the Spanish tried to establish settlements along the

coast, but battles with the Native American inhabitants led to their retreat, and it wasn't until 1670 that a permanent settlement was established, by the English this time, near present-day Charleston. The colony – one of the original thirteen colonies – was called Carolina, after King Charles I;

in 1729, after nearly two decades of disagreement over land ownership between the settlers, it was divided into two royal colonies, North and South Carolina. South Caroline quickly grew prosperous; its harbors made it a thriving trade center, and its fertile Low Country was ideal for agriculture. As more settlers arrived from Europe, they

began to establish plantations, cultivating rice and indigo crops on a large scale. This led to huge numbers of slaves being brought over from Africa; unfortunately, slave labor was the driving force behind South Carolina's economic success, and by the middle of the century, African slaves made up the majority of the colony's population. At the same time, smaller farms and traders were settling in the rest of the territory, steadily pushing the remaining native tribes further and further west.

By the beginning of the American Revolution, South Carolina was one of the most prosperous colonies in America. Rich merchants and plantation owners formed a strong governing class, and contributed many leaders to the fight for independence from Britain. More

Revolutionary War battles and skirmishes – over 200 of them -- were fought in South Carolina than anywhere else in America, and finally, after years of war and turmoil, South Carolina ratified the United States Constitution in 1788, and became the eighth state to enter the union. Today, some of the historic battle sites are marked with statues and museums, and if you are a lover of history you can combine a visit to a state park with a little Revolutionary War education.

The years following the war were a time of growth and prosperity for the state; the invention of the cotton gin allowed cotton to become a major crop for its upcountry farmers, and the new capital city – Columbia – was founded in the state's center, shifting some of the political power away from the wealthy landowners of the low

country. However, in spite of their newly-won independence from Britain and economic successes, there was a growing dissatisfaction with the federal government – particularly its tariff policies – and by the winter of 1860 these tensions reached a

climax. Unhappiness over free trade restrictions and calls for the abolition of slavery led to South Carolina being the first of the Southern states to secede from the union. In the spring of 1861, Confederate troops fired on Fort Sumter in Charleston Harbor, and the Civil War had begun.

The Civil War and its aftermath were, of course, devastating for South Carolina. Nearly one-fifth of its white male population was killed, and the economy was shattered. And finally, in 1865, General Sherman dealt the final blow – marching his troops

through the state, setting fires the burned down the plantations and most of the city of Columbia. The Reconstruction period that followed was, unsurprisingly, full of social, economic, and political upheaval. Former white leaders suddenly found *themselves lacking money or power, and the large population of freed slaves were seeking to improve their own economic and political positions. White conservatives were able to regain political power once more after federal troops were withdrawn in 1877, but the economy continued to suffer; cotton prices had plummeted and the old plantation system was dead. As the century drew to a close, populist reforms*

brought still more power to small white farmers, but left African Americans increasingly segregated and disenfranchised. The beginning of the 20th century saw the beginnings of economic recovery, first through the developing textile industry, and then various other manufactured goods. Other wounds took a bit longer to heal, but the civil rights movement of the 1960s brought a relatively peaceful end to segregation and legal discrimination, and the '70s saw three African Americans

WELCOME TO SOUTH CAROLINA

STACEY BREITBERG, EDITOR-AT-LARGE

elected to the state legislature, with many others to serve in state and local offices in the years since.

These days, South Carolina is a popular tourist destination, offering a wide variety of sights and activities. Its beaches attract sun-worshipping visitors – the Grand Strand, which stretches for 60 miles, is one of the most popular tourist destinations in the country – while kayaking enthusiasts love to take a trip down the Edisto River Canoe & Kayak Trail, which covers 66 miles of the Edisto River. There are also things you might not expect – like the Riverbanks Zoological Park, in Columbia, which is home to over 2000 animals, all in recreated natural habitats with no cages, bars, or

barriers. Or the largest Gingko farm in the world, which happens to be in the city of Sumter. In between beach-going, hiking mountain trails, visiting state parks, and just seeing the sights, there are also plenty of opportunities for good eating. Of course you'll find favorite snacks like boiled peanuts and peaches – South Carolina is proud of its peach industry, and holds an annual peach festival in the summertime; if you happen to stop in Gaffney, they even have an elevated water tower in the shape of a peach! – but there's a lot more than that. The Lowcountry offers many op-

portunities to try traditional Gullah cuisine – and learn about the history of the culture, and appreciate the survival and tenacity of the slave labor force responsible for the success of the state; consider trying some chicken bog, or Hoppin' John. You

can have the famous Southern meat-three-and-tea combination – sweet tea is South Carolina's official hospitality beverage, after all – or a simple BBQ pork sandwich. There are fresh seafood meals complete with a waterfront view – try some shrimp and grits or a hot bowl of she-crab soup. You can tour – and taste – your way through local wineries or spend an afternoon sitting in the sunshine, enjoying some locally brewed beer. With so many great options, you can't really go wrong…and if you miss something this time, it will just give you a fine excuse to come back again soon.

PALMETTO-TREE, AND OLD CUSTOM-HOUSE, AT CHARLESTON, SOUTH CAROLINA.

WELCOME TO SOUTH CAROLINA
STACEY BREITBERG, EDITOR-AT-LARGE

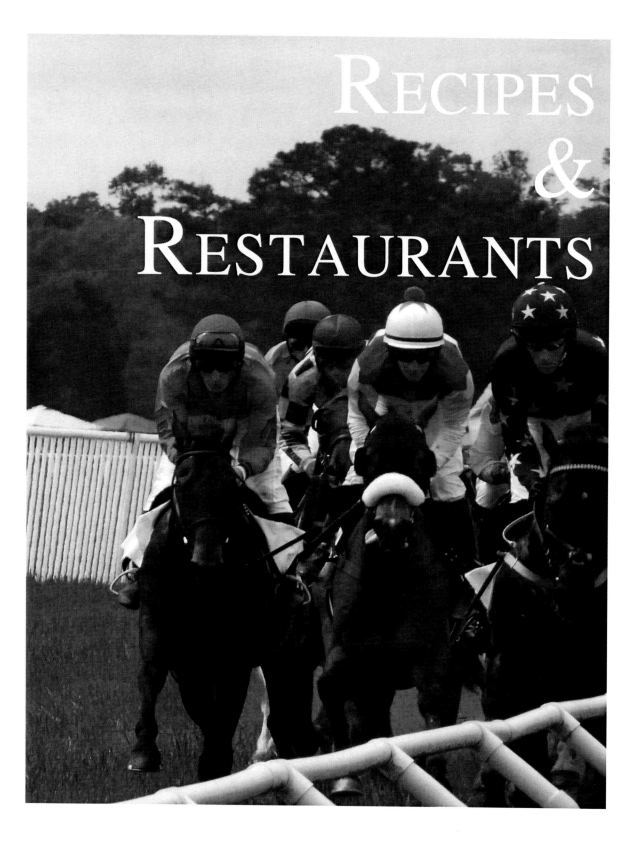

RECIPES
&
RESTAURANTS

5 Cheese Mac

Signature Tastes of SOUTH CAROLINA

3 slices American cheese
2 C. parmesan cheese
6 oz. Fontana cheese
6 oz. sharp cheddar cheese
3 oz. cream cheese
2 tsp garlic, chopped
2 tsp shallots, chopped
½ qt. heavy cream
½ qt. half & half
5 lbs cooked elbow noodles
Salt & pepper to taste

1. Lightly sweat the garlic and shallots.

2. Add the cream, half & half and cream cheese. Slurry to thicken.

3. Remove from heat and add the cheeses (reserving some). Blend with hand mixer and strain.

4. Add cooked elbow noodles. Place in a butter casserole dish.

5. Top with left over cheese and bake at 350°F for 20 minutes uncovered.

17 NORTH ROADSIDE KITCHEN
3563 HIGHWAY 17 NORTH, MOUNT PLEASANT

"This is a recipe that my Sous Chef, Danial Justice and I experimented with for several weeks until we finally came up with the perfect blend of cheeses. It's the best mac and cheese I have ever eaten."
Chef Brannon Flories

SHELLFISH A LA NICOISE

Signature Tastes of SOUTH CAROLINA

Roasted Garlic:
8 bulbs garlic
Vegetable oil

Shrimp & Scallops a la Nicoise:
¼ C. heavy cream
1 tsp parmesan cheese
5 diver scallops
5 shrimp 26/30 or larger, peeled & deveined
6 oz. penne pasta, cooked
3 oz. roasted garlic
½ bag thin green beans, blanched & finely chopped
4 nicoise olives
¼ C. sun dried tomatoes, chopped
2 oz. vegetable oil
Kosher salt for seasoning

Roasted Garlic:
1. Place garlic in baking dish or sauté pan. Cover in vegetable oil and roast in the oven at 425°F for 15 minutes.

2. Once mixture is done, remove the garlic bulbs, place in food processor or blender and blend until the mixture becomes smooth.

Shrimp & Scallops a la Nicoise:
1. In a large sauté pan, add vegetable oil and sear scallops and shrimp. Season with kosher salt.

2. Once the scallops and shrimp have a nice light brown color, flip and add pasta, tomatoes, olives and green beans.

3. Add the roasted garlic puree followed by the cream and reduce to a thick Alfredo consistency. Finish with some fresh parmesan cheese.

39 RUE DE JEAN
39 JOHN STREET, CHARLESTON

"....shellfish are the prime cause of the decline of morals and the adaptation of an extravagant lifestyle. Indeed of the whole realm of Nature the sea is in many ways the most harmful to the stomach, with its great variety of dishes and tasty fish."
Pliny the Elder (A.D. 23-79)

PEACH CRÈME BRULEE

With a focus on gracious Southern hospitality and fresh local cuisine, we've been providing our guests with a uniquely "Charleston" dining experience for almost a quarter of a century. In a town renowned for fine restaurants, 82 Queen has not only kept pace with strong competition, we've gained high marks for our unique approach to the menu of one of the nation's premiere dining destinations. Authentic Lowcountry cuisine, coupled with an award-winning wine list make dining at 82 Queen an incomparable experience.

Peach Puree:
3 SC peaches

Crème Brulee:
1 C. peach puree
1 C. heavy cream, heated to almost a simmer
9 egg yolks
½ C. sugar, plus 6 Tbsp for topping
1 tsp cinnamon
¾ tsp pure vanilla extract
Pinch of salt

Peach Puree:
1. Peel, remove seed and puree in blender. Use enough peaches to make 1 cup of puree.

Crème Brulee:
1. With a whisk, combine yolks, sugar, vanilla, cinnamon and salt until blended.

2. Temper warm crème into yolk mixture.

3. Add peach puree then strain through a fine mesh sieve.

4. Pour into 6 ounce ramekins and place in a water bath. Tip: Add hot water to your pan once you've placed them in the oven.

5. Cook at 325°F for about 30-40 minutes, or until custard is set. Custard should have a slight jiggle when set.

6. Let custard cool to room temperature and then refrigerate overnight.

To serve: Sprinkle 1 Tbsp of sugar on each custard and caramelize the sugar with a propane torch. Slowly rotate custard to melt and color the sugar as evenly as possible.

Signature Tastes of SOUTH CAROLINA

82 QUEEN
82 QUEEN STREET, CHARLESTON

"An apple is an excellent thing – until you have tried a peach."
George du Maurier (1834-1896)

Bacon Wrapped Mako Shark with Jamaican Rum BBQ Sauce

Formerly The Market – a one-stop shop for fresh products, meats, and seafood used to create mouth-watering, homemade meals by local residents – it's no wonder that A.W Shucks's is the mecca of delicious seafood in Charleston and quite possibly, the state of South Carolina. After having undergone massive changes to the menu by Executive Chef Mike Jackson, the final order up at our restaurant includes a diverse menu of classic Charleston tradition inspired foods such as crab cakes, seafood casseroles, fried shrimp, oysters, and a true (and quite rare!) major, raw oyster bar.

Marinade:
- 1 C. olive oil
- 1 C. pineapple juice
- 1 oz. garlic powder
- 1 oz. cumin
- 1 oz. chili powder
- 1 oz. cayenne pepper
- 1 oz. onion powder
- 1 oz. cilantro, chopped
- Salt & pepper to taste

BBQ Sauce:
- 2 C. Dark Jamaican Rum
- 4 Tbsp unsalted butter
- 1 large yellow onion, chopped
- 4 cloves garlic, chopped
- 2 C. ketchup
- 3 Tbsp tomato paste
- 1 12-oz. can Dr. Pepper®
- ½ C. cider vinegar
- ⅓ C. Worcestershire sauce
- 1 C. dark brown sugar
- 2 tsp Ancho or New Mexican chili powder
- 1 tsp white pepper
- 1 tsp kosher salt

Shark:
- 2 lbs Mako Shark (cut into 5 oz. steaks)
- 5 slices apple wood smoke bacon
- 15 toothpicks

Marinade:
1. Blend all ingredients and set aside.

Jamaican Rum BBQ Sauce:
1. Blend all ingredients and set aside.

Shark:
1. Wrap the bacon around the edge of the shark and stick a tooth pick in the bacon to hold it against the fish.

2. Place in the marinade for 3 hours.

3. Remove shark from the marinade and place the shark on the grill.

4. Grill for 3 minutes and 30 seconds then flip and grill for 4 more minutes.

5. Baste with Jamaican Rum BBQ sauce.

"One sustainable seafood item that lets me know I live on the coast of South Carolina is Mako shark. When in season, Mako is hard to come by due to popularity but my crew loves to fish so for us we seem to find it. A great marinade is the key to enhancing the flavor. Add the Rum BBQ sauce and you have created a fish classic courtesy of the coast of South Carolina."
Chef Mike Jackson

23

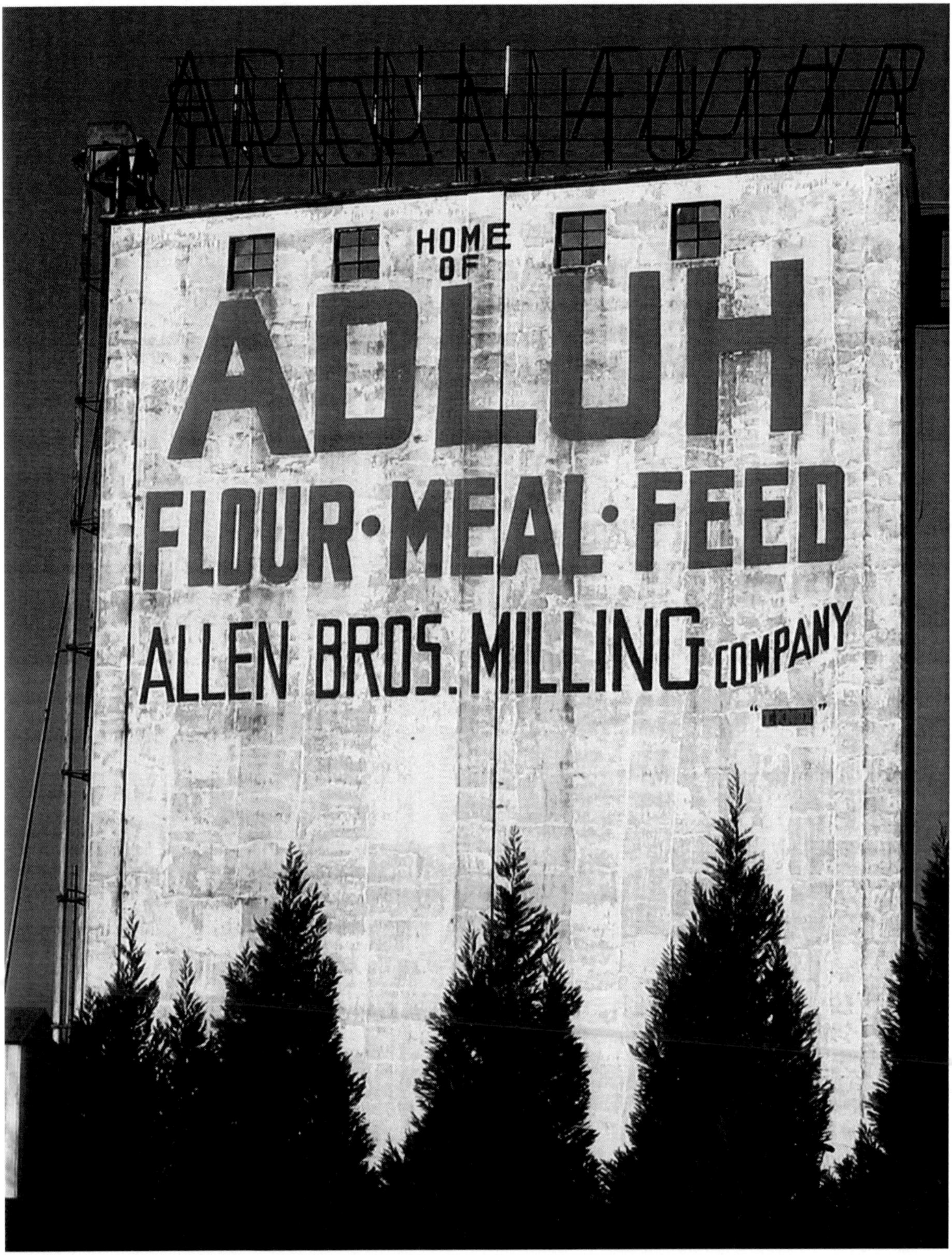
HOME OF
ADLUH
FLOUR·MEAL·FEED
ALLEN BROS. MILLING COMPANY

JACK'S CROCK POT CHEESE YELLOW GRITS

Signature Tastes of SOUTH CAROLINA

The Adluh Flour mill stands tall in the heart of Columbia, South Carolina's Congaree Vista, and has been owned and operated by the Allen family from Wadesboro, NC, since June 1926. Today, J. B. Allen's grandson Jack Edgerton, is the longest-serving President and CEO of Adluh Flour. Beloved for his acts of community service as much as for his products of uncompromising quality, Jack is also well-known for making a mean pot o'grits. Anybody who knows Jack knows that he has always been happy to share his recipe with anyone who asks, and now he's happy to share it with you.

*1 C. Adluh Stone-ground Yellow Grits
3 C. hot water
1 C. milk, heavy cream or half &-half (may use just water)
1 pinch salt (may substitute ¼ - ½ chicken bullion cube)
1 pinch sugar
¼ stick margarine
¾ C. cheese, shredded
1-2 tsp Texas Pete*

1. Add hot water to crock pot, set on high, and then add grits. Stir and remove floating particles (corn bran) with a ladle or spoon if desired.

2. Cook on high, stirring every 15-20 minutes. After 1 ½ to 2 hours, add milk or cream and continue stirring.

3. Wait 30-40 minutes and then add cheese and hot sauce. Add margarine, sugar and salt/bullion at any time. Reduce heat and simmer until ready to serve. Cooking time can be reduced or increased depending on the consistency desired.

Lid should be kept on pot during the entire cooking cycle. The longer they cook, the better they taste! For standard grits, omit the cheese and hot sauce.

Makes 4-6 servings

804 ½ GERVAIS STREET, COLUMBIA

ADLUH FLOUR

"I like to think I am well-mannered. If I have the option at a breakfast place, I'll go with the grits. That's how Southern I am."
Michael C. Hall, Actor

SHRIMP & GRITS

On a picturesque lagoon in Palmetto Dunes, Alexander's has been an Island tradition since 1977. Choose from over 100 hand selected wines to compliment the freshest seafood and hand trimmed steaks and enjoy the vintage Harley Davidson collection.

Andouille Cream Sauce:
2 Tbsp butter
2 Tbsp flour
1 lb Andouille sausage, large diced
1 ½ C. heavy or whipping cream
1 ½ C. half & half
1 Tbsp garlic, minced
⅓ C. blackening spice
½ tsp leaf thyme
1 C. parmesan cheese
½ tsp salt

Shrimp:
9 large shrimp, peeled & deveined
1 red bell pepper, julienned
2 tsp butter

Cheddar Grits:
Grits
Chicken stock
Cream
3 dashes of Tabasco
1 tsp garlic powder
Eggs
Flour
Plain bread crumbs

Andouille Cream Sauce:
1. Heat butter in a saucepan over medium heat. Add sausage and sauté for 3-4 minutes.
2. Add flour and blend with a wire whisk. Add garlic and cook 1 minute more.
3. Add remaining ingredients, whisking together to stir out all lumps; cook until thickened. Taste sauce before adding salt; some blackening spices are very salty.

Shrimp:
1. Sauté shrimp and pepper in butter until almost cooked.
2. Add Andouille Cream Sauce; bring to a simmer. If sauce is too thick, thin with a little chicken stock or cream.
3. Divide shrimp equally onto 4 plates and serve with cheddar grits.

Cheddar Grits:
1. Using your favorite quick grit recipe, measure the appropriate amount of grits to make 2 cups. Instead of water, substitute ½ chicken stock and ½ cream to equal the amount of liquid called for in the recipe. Add Tabasco and garlic powder and cook grits according to recipe.
2. Pour finished grits into a small baking dish or loaf pan. Let cook until firm.
3. Cut into 4 equal parts. Roll in flour, egg wash and plain bread crumbs.
4. Pan fry until golden brown and crispy.

76 QUEENS FOLLY ROAD, HILTON HEAD ISLAND

ALEXANDER'S

"I think somebody should come up with a way to breed a very large shrimp. That way, you could ride him, then, after you're camped at night, you could eat him. How about it science?"
Jack Handey, American humorist

FRIED GREEN TOMATOES

Dishes are based on traditional Southern cuisine, with Chef Curry Martin's own personal twist. Our menu changes seasonally and offers simple, but flavorful dishes with ingredients sourced from the best local suppliersNever overbearing, but always helpful, our knowledgeable and attentive staff is trained to ensure the time you spend at Aspen Grille is absolutely enjoyable and truly memorable. Aspen Grille is the perfect place for a quiet night out for two or a lively group event. You'll find that our exceptional service and attention to detail will make any occasion all that you hoped it would be.

*1 green tomato, chilled
& sliced approximately
¼" thick
Pancetta bacon,
sliced thin
3 oz. parmesan cheese
2 eggs
2 C. seasoned flour
Lump crab (optional)*

1. Heat preferred cooking oil to 350°F.

2. Dredge chilled tomato slices in eggs and flour, making sure it is covered all over.

3. Place in hot oil and fry until golden brown, turning to ensure evenness on all sides. Once golden, remove from fryer and pat off excess oil.

4. Place on tray and add 1 slice of bacon and 1 oz. of cheese to each slice.

5. Place in preheated 350°F oven until cheese is melted.

6. Top with lump crab if desired. Serve with preferred sauce.

Makes 3-5 slices depending on size of tomato.

Signature Tastes of SOUTH CAROLINA

5101 NORTH KINGS HIGHWAY, MYRTLE BEACH

ASPEN GRILLE

"Oh, what I wouldn't give for a plate of fried green tomatoes like we used to have at the cafe. Ooh!"
Jessica Tandy as Ninny Threadgoode in Fried Green Tomatoes

BEACON DRIVE-IN PIMENTO CHEESE

SOUTH CAROLINA

Signature Tastes of

It's a Southern tradition to eat at The Beacon Drive-In. You'll be greeted by Smiles-A-Plenty and served with Service-A-Plenty. Famous for our Chili Cheese A-Plenty, a chili cheeseburger on a bun buried on a plate underneath piles of sweet onion rings and French fried potatoes and the great drive-in tea of the South – generously sweetened, laced with a touch of lemon, served over a pack of shaved ice. We sell more tea than any other single restaurant in the US! The Beacon Drive-In is one of the few drive-in restaurant legends remaining that offers curb service.

1 lb American cheese
(1) 4 oz. jar pimientos, drained
2 Tbsp Duke's mayonnaise

1. Grind up the cheese and pimentos in a food processor until almost smooth, but with some small pieces of pimento visible.

2. Scrape into a bowl and stir in the mayo.

255 JOHN B. WHITE SR. BOULEVARD, SPARTANBURG

THE BEACON DRIVE-IN

"Thank God for tea! What would the world do without tea? How did it exist? I am glad I was not born before tea."
Sydney Smith, English writer (1771-1845)

Barbeque Grilled Meatloaf

We have deep roots in the Southern communities we've served since 1961, and we dedicate everything we do to providing our shoppers in those communities with freshness, variety and unmatched savings. In an age where individuals and families have so many choices but less and less time, we've created a local grocery store where shoppers can get everything they need with hundreds of ways to reduce the money they spend. BI-LO's strong values and commitment to our communities drive us to work hard to give back through our charitable fundraisers and community events.

1 lb Laura's 96% Lean Ground Beef
½ small onion, finely chopped
1 C. Southern Home® plain dried breadcrumbs
1 egg, lightly beaten
1/3 C. Stubb's® Bar-B-Q Sauce
Southern Home® vegetable cooking spray
¼ C. Stubb's® Bar-B-Q Sauce

1. Combine ground beef, onion, breadcrumbs, egg and 1/3 C. barbeque sauce in a large bowl. Shape into a loaf.

2. Wrap in aluminum foil coated with cooking spray and chill 15 minutes in the freezer.

3. Poke fork-size holes on both sides of the foil.

4. Grill meatloaf in foil package, covered with grill lid, over medium-high heat 10-15 minutes on each side, or until a meat thermometer inserted into thickest portion registers 155°F.

5. Open foil and spoon remaining ¼ C. barbeque sauce over meatloaf. Cover with aluminum foil for 5-10 minutes to heat through.

Signature Tastes of SOUTH CAROLINA

MULTIPLE LOCATIONS ACROSS THE STATE

BI-LO

"We're not going to do the usual giveaways, gimmicks or stamps. We're just going to offer discounted prices to our shoppers."
Frank Outlaw, Founder,
upon buying what would ultimately become Bi-Lo in 1961

33

CANDY OF THE SEA

Brother and sister team, Jason and Allison Clark bring to Historic Greer a unique and creative dining experience. Come in and share their pride in choosing only the finest ingredientsthat make up their "Southeastern with a Twist" cuisine. BIN112 offers an extensive wine list and full bar to complement every dish and bring out the Epicurean in all of you. BIN112 strives to be one of the friendliest restaurants in downtown Greer, dedicating itself to creating a pleasurable and comfortable experience for all of its guests.

1 ½ lbs sea scallops,lg
kosher salt
⅛ cup coconut milk
1 pinch
Chinese fried garlic
¼ cup all-purpose flour
Kosher salt, pepper
2 tbsp unsalted butter
Carolina Gold Pilaf
1 slice bacon, ½ " cubes
¼ tsp extra virgin olive oil
⅓ sweet onion, finely diced
1 clove garlic, thinly sliced
1 bay leaf
½ tsp crushed red pepper
1 thyme sprig
3 cups chicken stock, low salt
Salt to taste
1 cup Carolina Gold
1 plum tomato, halved, seeded and diced
2 ounces okra, trimmed & sliced crosswise ¼" thick

1. Rinse and drain scallops; pat dry with paper towels.
2. Dip in coconut milk and fried garlic, sprinkle with flour and pepper.
3. Heat 2 tablespoons butter in large skillet over medium-high heat. Add scallops; sauté until browned outside and just opaque in center, about 2 minutes per side.
4. Top each scallop with 1 tsp chili sauce and a drop of cilantro pesto. Serve around Sofrito collard greens (see page 134) and Carolina gold rice pilaf.

Carolina Gold Pilaf
1. In a large, heavy casserole, cook the bacon in the olive oil over moderately high heat until crisp, about 5 minutes. Using a slotted spoon, remove the bacon; reserve it for another use.
2. Add the onion, garlic, bay leaf, thyme sprig and crushed red pepper to the casserole and cook over moderately low heat, stirring, until the onion is softened, about 5 minutes.
3. Add the chicken stock and 1 1/2 teaspoons of salt and bring to a boil. Add the rice and return to a boil, stirring.
4. Cover and cook over low heat until the rice is barely tender and still quite soupy, about 12 minutes.
5. Add the tomato and okra to the casserole and cook until it is just tender, about 4 minutes.

Note: chili dipping sauce and cilantro pesto are both available in the condiment section of your grocer

BIN II2 ON TRADE STREET

II2 TRADE STREET, GREER

"Our restaurant is located in a 100-year-old historic building…our only complaint for three years of business is the noise…most of our customers say it is the humming of a good restaurant…"
Jason Clark
Owner

SUSHI NACHOS

Black Marlin offers the Island's largest selection of fresh-caught fish, seafood and delicious hand-cut steaks, all in a relaxing Key West atmosphere. Located dockside at Palmetto Bay Marina, you can dine indoors or outdoors on the expansive patio. Enjoy appetizers like our award-winning Sushi Nachos from the waterside World Famous Hurricane Bar. The newly expanded Hurricane Bar also features Fat Tuesday Frozen Daiquiris. Join us – Black Marlin invites you to enjoy the freshest seafood on the Island.

Wasabi Aioli:
2 Tbsp mayo
1 tsp wasabi paste
1 tsp lime juice

Soy Chile Vinaigrette:
1 Tbsp rice wine vinegar
1 tsp sesame oil
1 Tbsp green onions, chopped
1 Tbsp garlic Chile sauce
¼ tsp fresh garlic, chopped
1 tsp soy sauce
Black pepper to taste

Sushi Nachos:
4 fried wonton crisps (2 wontons cut in half)
4 slices Cajun seasoned tuna
3 Tbsp Soy Chile Vinaigrette
Wasabi Aioli
Pickled ginger
Sesame seeds (black & white)
Sliced avocado

Wasabi Aioli:
1. Mix all ingredients with a whisk

Soy Chile Vinaigrette:
1. Mix all ingredients with a whisk

Sushi Nachos:
1. Sear tuna on each side for 30 seconds and place in refrigerator to cool before slicing.

2. Place a wonton on your favorite plate and place a slice of avocado, slice of seared tuna and pickled ginger on each wonton. Drizzle with Soy Chile Vinaigrette and Wasabi Aioli and top with sesame seeds.

3. Continue to build in the above order for each wonton. Quantities of sauce and ingredients are subject to personal taste.

THE BLACK MARLIN BAYSIDE GRILL
86 HELMSMAN WAY SUITE 103, HILTON HEAD ISLAND

"In Mexico we have a word for sushi: bait."
Jose Simon

BLUE MARLIN SHRIMP & GRITS

Stretching from Savannah to the South, and Georgetown to the North, the Lowcountry is resplendent with the bounties of the sea and coastal marshlands. We're proud to bring the flavors of this fare to you at the Blue Marlin. As you enjoy our signature dishes, you'll experience the finest blend of African, West Indian and Caribbean flavors. Continuing in the vein of this delectable cuisine, we also feature many dishes with the Cajun and Creole influence of the Louisiana Delta, a region just as rich in unique flavors and seasonings as the Lowcountry.

Grits:
½ gallon chicken stock, or water & bouillon cubes to equal 1 gallon
1 oz. kosher salt
½ tsp white pepper
14 oz. stone ground Adluh grits
1 C. heavy cream
1 C. whole milk

Tasso Gravy:
2 oz. butter
3 oz. Tasso ham, finely diced
2 oz. all-purpose flour
1 ½ C. chicken stock, hot
1 tsp kosher salt

Andouille Sausage & Shrimp:
Andouille sausage
Shrimp, peeled & deveined
2 oz. butter
Salt, pepper & Old Bay
Fresh parsley

Grits:
1. In a heavy bottom stock pot, bring chicken stock and salt & pepper to a boil. Whisk in grits and reduce heat to medium-low. Mix steadily until grits and liquid are combined. Cook for 30-45 minutes on medium-low heat stirring frequently to prevent grits from burning to bottom of the pot. Once the grits begin to soften to the bite, whisk in milk and cream. Taste and adjust seasoning if needed. If you have leftovers you can pour into a shallow pan and refrigerate overnight and make grit cakes the next day. Cut grits with a cookie cutter, dredge in seasoned flour and pan fry on a griddle or sauté pan in butter or olive oil.

Tasso Gravy
1. In a sauce pot, melt butter and sauté the ham for 2 minutes to release flavors. Whisk in flour and cook for 5 minutes stirring frequently to make roux. Slowly add hot chicken stock to the roux and whisk continuously to prevent lumps of flour. Simmer for 5 minutes and taste.

Andouille Sausage & Shrimp:
1. For the shrimp and sausage we use Carolina or gulf shrimp, which ever we can get, and serve 4 oz. per person for lunch and 8 oz. per person for dinner. We also sauté diced Andoullie sausage with our shrimp to add some spice.
2. In sauté pan, heat 2 oz. butter until sizzling in pan. Add sausage (4 pieces per person) and let cook for 1 minute so the sausage releases its fat and then add shrimp. Sauté the shrimp until they are translucent and then season with salt, pepper and Old Bay.

To serve: Place 6 oz. grits in a bowl. Top with 4-8 oz. shrimp and 1 oz. sausage followed by 4 oz. of Tasso gravy. Garnish with parsley. Enjoy.

"Anyway, like I was sayin', shrimp is the fruit of the sea. You can barbecue it, boil it, broil it, bake it, sauté it. Dey's uh, shrimp-kabobs, shrimp Creole, shrimp gumbo. Pan fried, deep fried, stir-fried. There's pineapple shrimp, lemon shrimp, coconut shrimp, pepper shrimp, shrimp soup, shrimp stew, shrimp salad, shrimp and potatoes, shrimp burger, shrimp sandwich. That- that's about it."
Bubba, from the movie Forrest Gump

THE
BOATHOUSE
At Breach Inlet

BOATHOUSE SHRIMP & GRITS

Signature Tastes of **SOUTH CAROLINA**

The structure now known as "The Boathouse at Breach Inlet" was originally a ramshackle bait shop on the southeast corner of Isle of Palms overlooking the water. We introduced a new concept to the menu when we first opened in 1997, giving guests the opportunity to choose from up to half a dozen types of the freshest fish to be found, and an equal number of preparation styles thereby quickly becoming known by locals and tourists alike as the best spot for waterfront dining in Charleston! Our current offerings are better than ever with a passionate, close knit crew running the kitchen.

**4 Tbsp vegetable or canola oil
3 lbs shrimp, 26/30 count or larger, peeled & deveined
1 lb Andouille sausage, sliced
3 cloves garlic, finely minced
1 each small red, yellow, green bell pepper, julienned
1 large red onion, sliced
1 ½ C. tomatoes, chopped
1 Tbsp Boathouse Blackening Seasoning, or your favorite
1 C. clam juice, vegetable or chicken stock
1 ½ C. Green Tabasco Cream Sauce
5 green onions, sliced
6 C. favorite cooked grits**

1. Heat oil in a large skillet over medium-high heat until smoking.

2. Add the shrimp followed by the sausage and garlic, sautéing for 1 minute.

3. Add the peppers and onions and sauté for 1 more minute.

4. Add the chopped tomatoes and blackening seasoning.

5. Add the claim juice to thin out the sauce (you may not need to use the entire cup).

6. Place shrimp mixture over a bed of grits and drizzle with Boathouse Green Tabasco Cream Sauce. Garnish with green onions.

"Our slogan, 'Simply Fresh Seafood,' was and is our mission statement. As my cousin David Farrow says, 'Good food is the difference between living and living well."
Richard Stoney, Owner

BBQ PULLED PORK SLIDERS

A unique restaurant and bar located in Coligny Plaza just off the beach. Offering fresh and local Lowcounty ingredients paired with craft beers, wines and cocktails that are "The Bomb". Come in and check us out!

Maw Maw Slaw:
2 heads Napa cabbage
1 head collard greens
4 carrots
1 bunch green onions
1 red onion
Maw Maw Dressing:
¼ C. blended oil
¼ C. white vinegar
4 tsp sugar
½ C. Creole mustard
1 tsp garlic, chopped
¼ tsp black pepper
¼ tsp Cajun spice
1 C. mayo
BBQ Sauce:
4 cloves garlic
¼ tsp salt
2 C. Coca Cola®
2 C. Dr. Pepper®
1 ½ C. ketchup
¼ C. cider vinegar
2 Tbsp Worcestershire sauce
1 Tbsp chipotle powder
1 tsp black pepper
1 tsp Buffalo Sauce
¼ tsp All Spice
1 ½ tsp lemon juice
BBQ Pulled Pork Sliders:
1 pork butt (Boston Butt)
2 C. Pork Rub
1 qt. Coca Cola®
1 qt. beer (West Brook IPA)
6 stalks celery, diced
4 carrots, diced
1 yellow onion, cut into rings
Sliced Pickles
30 Broche Slider Buns
Butter, melted

Pork Rub:
½ C. sugar   ½ C. garlic powder
½ C. brown sugar   ½ C. chili powder
½ C. paprika   ¼ C. cumin
¼ C. coriander   3 Tbsp salt
3 Tbsp black pepper 3 Tbsp oregano
2 tsp cayenne pepper

Mix all ingredients. You'll have extra pork rub to use for later recipes, marinades etc.

Maw Maw Slaw:
1. Slice all vegetables very thin and mix in bowl.
Maw Maw Dressing:
1. Mix all ingredients. Add to Maw Maw Slaw and then mix together. Serve on top of BBQ Pulled Pork on Slider.
BBQ Sauce:
1. Mix everything except lemon juice and simmer for 2 hours on medium heat. Once thick, add lemon juice.

BBQ Pulled Pork Sliders:
1. Place onion rings on top of carrots and celery to hold pork above vegetables in a roasting pan. Rub pork with 2 C. pork rub. Sear on a flat top or frying pan on all sides and then place on top of onions in roasting pan. Mix Coca Cola® and beer together and pour over pork. Cover tight with aluminum foil and bake at 450°F for 4 hours.
2. After cooked, remove from liquid and remove the bone and fat cap. Use two forks and shred against the grain. Mix pork with 2 C. BBQ Sauce.
3. Cut Brioche buns in half, butter each inside and sear them off. Put one sliced pickle on the bottom bun, add pork and top with Maw Maw Slaw. Serve with a side of BBQ Sauce. Makes 30+ Mini Sliders.

BOMBORAS GRILLE & CHILL BAR
101 A/B POPE AVENUE COLIGNY PLAZA, HILTON HEAD ISLAND

"Barbecue is a guy thing, a throwback to the spit-roasted woolly mammoth perhaps. It tends to be written about today (and debated in endless detail) like a sporting event, which in fact it has become: thousands of tiny local competitions are rapidly giving way to several major barbecue leagues, with their own playoffs, world series - and six-figure purses."
Molly O'Neill, 'American Food Writing' (2007)

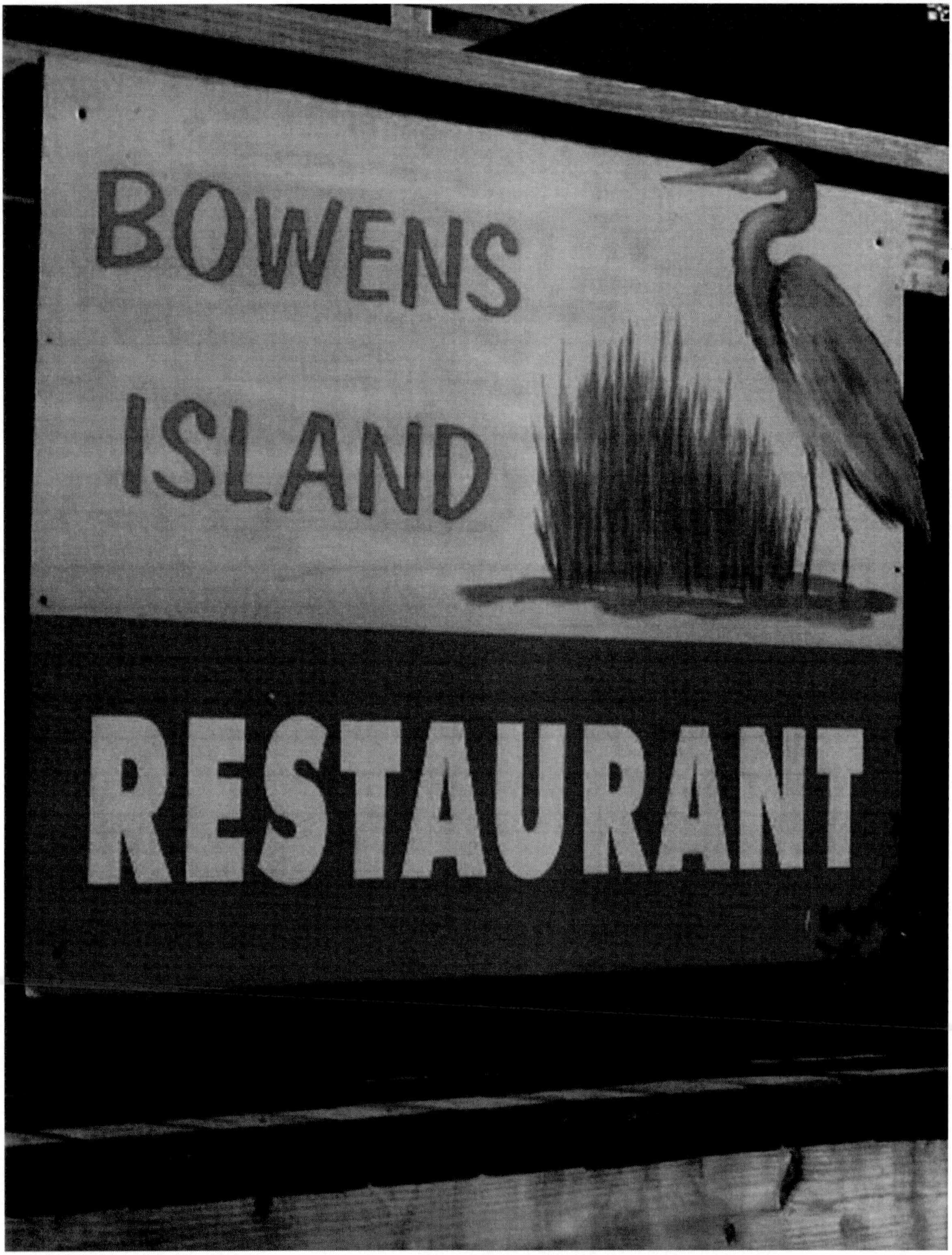
BOWENS
ISLAND
RESTAURANT

FROGMORE STEW

Founded by May and Jimmy Bowen in 1946, their grandson Robert Barber continues the tradition today. Located at the tip of a 13-acre island, the restaurant is famous for its roasted oysters, fried shrimp, rustic atmosphere, 1946 Seeberg jukebox which plays a 78 record for a quarter, and its undisturbed views of river, marshes, islands, and wildlife. Featured in numerous national newspapers, magazines, and TV shows, as well as having received the James Beard Foundation Award in 2006 as an American Classic, Bowens Island is a unique dining experience which deserves to be enjoyed at least once.

2 lbs fresh shrimp, peeled & deveined
1 ½ – 2 lbs Hillshire Farms sausage
1 ½ lbs small red potatoes
6 ears corn, broken in half
3 Tbsp Old Bay seasoning
Dash of Texas Pete (optional)

1. Fill large pot ¼ full of water. Add Old Bay and Texas Pete.

2. When water starts to boil, add potatoes and cook about 10 minutes or until potatoes are easy to pierce with fork.

3. Add sausage and cook for about 5 minutes.

4. With the water still boiling, add the shrimp. Cut off heat and stir until the shrimp are a little pink. Drain.

The key to good Frogmore stew is to make certain not to overcook the shrimp. Because there is a lot of heat in the potatoes, corn, and sausage, the shrimp will continue to cook after you drain the stew.

Serves 6.

BOWEN'S ISLAND RESTAURANT
1200 LINCOLN STREET, CHARLESTON

"Does your tummy turn over when thinking about Frogmore Stew? Wondering how many more frogs are required for this South Carolina specialty? Relax, there are NO frogs in Frogmore Stew – in fact, it is more of an event than a dish. That is Southern cuisine the South Carolina way."
Discover South Carolina

CRAB CAKE DIJONNAISE

Chef Eric Masson, a French native, holds three French culinary degrees and has worked in many prestigious hotels and restaurants in Paris, London and New York. In 1998, Eric migrated to the USA and opened his first restaurant Ferrandi's in upstate New York followed by The Saratoga Lake Bistro in Saratoga Springs. Eric's culinary approach is creative yet simple with an emphasis on fresh, local products and dishes which are not only delicious but also healthy and natural. He specializes in "Low Country French Cuisine", which incorporate Southern style cooking with an added unique French twist.

Signature Tastes of SOUTH CAROLINA

THE BRENTWOOD RESTAURANT & WINE BISTRO
4269 LUCK AVENUE, LITTLE RIVER

Crab Cake:
1 lb lump crab meat, picked free of shells
1 medium onion, peeled & finely chopped
2 stalks celery, washed & finely chopped
1 Tbsp garlic, finely chopped
1 C. Panko
2 Tbsp whole grain Dijon mustard
1 C. mayo
½ lemon, juiced
2 Tbsp olive oil
1 tsp salt
½ tsp pepper
1 dash cayenne pepper
1 Tbsp chives or parsley, finely chopped

Sauce Dijonnaise:
½ C. heavy cream
2 Tbsp whole grain Dijon mustard

1. In medium saucepan, sauté onion and celery in olive oil for 3-4 minutes.

2. Add garlic and cook for 3 more minutes.

3. Remove from stove, transfer to mixing bowl and add mayo, Dijon mustard, lemon juice, cayenne pepper and salt & pepper.

4. Carefully fold in crab meat to preserve lump shape and add Panko to firm up consistency.

5. Heat olive oil in a large skillet over medium heat. When oil is hot, carefully place crab cakes, in batches, in pan and fry until browned, about 4-5 minutes.

6. In medium saucepan, boil cream and Dijon mustard for 3-4 minutes and set aside.

7. Serve crab cakes with Sauce Dijonnaise and garnish with chives or parsley.

"So if anybody wants to get me something, get me 60 crabs - one for each year. I don't want no diamonds, I don't want no shoes, I don't want no party. I want some crabs."
Patti LaBelle

DUCK BURRITOS

Located just off bustling Main Street, Café And Then Some brings you folksy satire, music and great food, blended with a personal touch by proprietors Bill and Susan Smith. Bill's better known on stage as Bubba. Susan's best known as Norma Jean, a big ole country and western star! Whether you're celebrating a birthday, anniversary or just looking for a great night out, we invite you to join us for an evening of both entertainment and great food at Café And Then Some.

Duck Burritos:
2 C. duck confit
2 C. sautéed duck
1 C. green bell pepper, julienned
1 C. onion, julienned
2 C. sharp cheddar, shredded
1 bunch cilantro, coarsely chopped
2 Tbsp cumin
3 Tbsp Ancho chili powder
1 Tbsp garlic
1 Tbsp granulated onion
1 tsp cayenne pepper
1 tsp salt
2 limes, juiced
⅓ C. canola oil
Corn Relish:
1 C. shoe peg corn
1 C. sour orange
1 bunch cilantro, coarsely chopped
1 red bell pepper, diced
1 green bell pepper, diced
1 jalapeno pepper, diced
1 Tbsp cumin
1 Tbsp Ancho chili powder
2 Tbsp hot sauce
¼ C. apple cider vinegar
Salt to taste

Duck Confit:
1. Reduce duck thighs and legs in their own fat on low to medium heat, rendering fat as you go. Set aside and allow to cool.

Duck Burritos:
1. Grill or sauté duck or chicken breast, cooking thoroughly but kept moist. Set aside and allow to cool.

2. Sauté bell pepper and onion until tender. Set aside and allow to cool.

3. Pull or julienne the cooked breasts and then mix with the confit, sautéed peppers, onions and cheddar cheese.

4. Mix spices thoroughly with canola oil and lime juice to make a marinade. Pour marinade over the breast mixture and refrigerate overnight.

Corn Relish:
1. Combine all ingredients and allow to marry overnight in refrigerator.

To serve: Roll the completed mixture into 5" flour tortillas. Can be served cold or microwaved for a few seconds to serve warm. Serve burritos topped with corn relish and sour cream.

CAFÉ AND THEN SOME
101 COLLEGE STREET, GREENVILLE

"If it looks like a duck, and quacks like a duck, we have at least to consider the possibility that we have a small aquatic bird of the family anatidae on our hands."
Douglas Adams, Writer

Cajun Kountry

COUNTRY-SOUTHERN SOUL FOOD FU

1382 B

Cajun Kountry Cafe

225-5590

COU

gum

etou

GATOR SMOKED RIBS

Cajun Kountry Café combines the best of southern and soul food country cooking with a Cajun/Creole twist. Chef Frisco creates classic dishes to order for all to enjoy. Our food is well complimented by the whimsical atmosphere. Colorful and creative could only describe the food at the Cajun Kountry Cafe. With a modest price and quality customer service, this food is sure to please all palates.

6 lbs Gator ribs
4 oz. your choice of
blackened seasoning
5 oz. Worcestershire
sauce
5 oz. brown sugar
2 oz. salt
4 oz. cumin
4 oz. chili powder
1 C. Marsala wine
2 C. water
1 C. red wine
3 oz. whiskey
Smoke chips

1. Soak smoke chips overnight in water.

2. Clean and separate the Gator ribs.

3. Coat ribs with the blackened seasoning, cumin, chili, salt and brown sugar rub.

4. Store and allow ribs to marinate in the refrigerator.

5. Light your own smoker as directed and smoke for 1 hour.

6. Preheat oven to 350°F.

7. Place ribs in a large baking pan and pour the Marsala wine, red wine, whiskey and Worcestershire sauce over the ribs.

8. Cover with plastic then with aluminum foil. Place in oven for 2 hours or until meat is fork tender from bones.

CAJUN KOUNTRY CAFÉ
1382 B. REMOUNT ROAD, NORTH CHARLESTON

"Not spicy, just right! Not Louisiana but Charleston, SC."
Chef Frisco

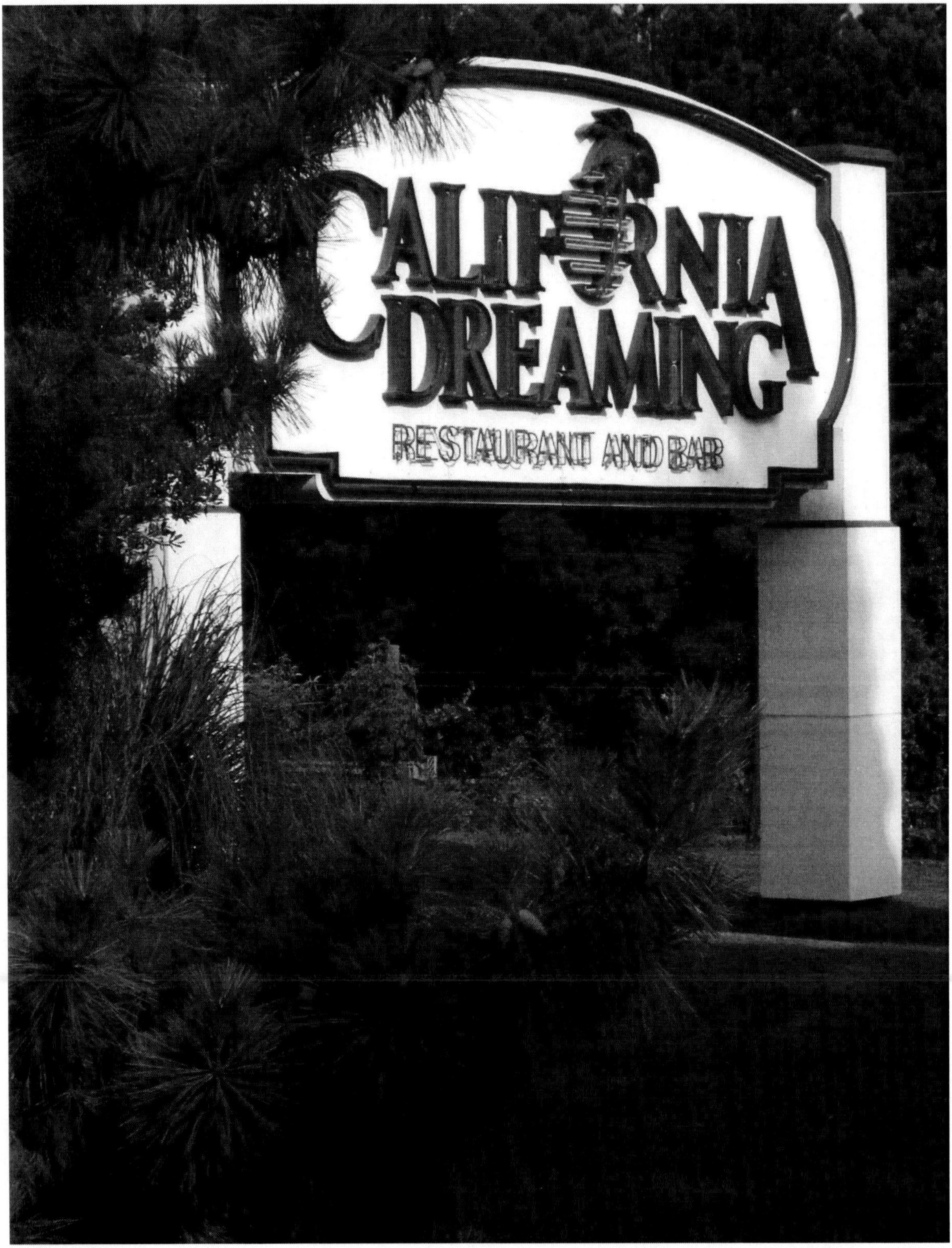
CALIFORNIA
DREAMING
RESTAURANT AND BAR

SEAFOOD NACHOS

California Dreaming opened its doors in 1984 in a historic railroad depot at Union Station in Columbia, South Carolina located right off the USC campus. "Make it Fresh and Make it Right". These two simple ideals make us the perfect place to enjoy a casual lunch or a special night out. Enjoy our Pittsburgh-style steaks, fall-off-the-bone baby back ribs or fresh seafood. Don't forget to try our award winning California Dreaming Salad. We always have huge portions, modest pricing and unbeatable American cuisine.

5 oz. or 50 chips
1 seafood nacho set
(Lobster cream sauce, salmon & southwest shrimp)

Cheese sauce:
2 oz. American cheese
2 oz. heavy cream

Pinch chopped parsley

Seafood nacho set:
2 oz. lobster base
4 oz. heavy cream
3 oz. salmon pieces, skin removed
3 oz. 31/40 shrimp
Cajun seasoning mix

Seafood Set:
1. Combine lobster base and heavy cream in a sauce pan over low heat. Cook, stirring constantly.

2. Add salmon, shrimp and Cajun seasoning mix (to taste). Cook until shrimp are done, about 5 minutes

Cheese Sauce:
1. Combine cheese and cream in a sauce pan over low heat until smooth.

Nachos:
1. Heat seafood nacho set in microwave for 2 minutes or until piping hot.

2. Place ½ of chips on plate and ladle 2 oz. cheese sauce over chips.

3. Add remaining chips and pour hot seafood set over cheese and chips.

4. Ladle remaining cheese sauce over seafood set.

5. Place dish under cheese melter until cheese is well browned. Sprinkle chopped parsley over entire dish.

Note: Cheese melter must be set on low heat in order to leave chips in long enough to heat thoroughly without burning.

"Why does Sea World have a seafood restaurant? I'm halfway through my fish burger and I realize, Oh my God....I could be eating a slow learner."
Lyndon B. Johnson, former President of the U.S.

SHRIMP & GRITS CUBAN STYLE (TAMAL EN CAZUELA CON CAMARONES)

Carlos Café is a family-owned Cuban restaurant created to give the Carolinas' palette an authentic taste of Cuba. Owners Joe and Flor Strollo are bringing a piece of Cuba's heritage, flavors and culture with their small eatery in a big way! Cuban food is a fusion of flavorful spices of Spanish, African, Chinese and Caribbean cuisines and our menu reads like a concise compendium of what Cuban cuisine lovers look for in comfort food. In the front is a small food display with stacked Cuban sandwiches and desserts. But what hits you first hopefully is our warmth; we're glad you're here.

Ingredients:

1 ½-2 lbs shrimp, peeled & deveined
2 C. polenta
4 oz. Spanish dry sausage (Chorizo)
4 oz. gouda cheese
½ large onion, diced
4 C. water
Salt to taste
1 tsp black pepper
2 tsp garlic powder
1 ½-2 C. milk
2 Tbsp olive oil
½ stick butter
1 oz. hot sauce
1-2 tsp minced garlic, or to taste
4-5 oz. of your favorite marinara sauce
½ small onion, minced
Parsley, chopped

1. Bring water to boil and add salt, pepper and powdered garlic.

2. Slowly add polenta and whisk constantly.

3. When thick, add milk, butter, and gouda cheese. Keep warm.

4. Warm up marinara sauce.

5. In a large skillet, sauté onion, minced garlic to taste and the Spanish dry sausage (Chorizo).

6. Add shrimp when onions are clear and cook until shrimps are fully cooked, about 3 minutes. Add marinara sauce till heated through.

7. Serve polenta in a medium size bowl. Add the marinara sauce, with the Spanish dry sauce (Chorizo) and 6-8 shrimp.

8. Garnish with chopped onion and parsley. Serve with fried sweet or green plantains and a small side salad of fresh crisp iceberg lettuce, tomato, cucumber and onion.

Pairing Suggestion: Sangria. A punch typical of Spain. It normally consists of a light – dry – young – high acid unoaked red wine with chopped or sliced fruit such as orange, lemon, lime, apple, peach, melon, berries, pineapple, grape and mango.

CARLOS CAFÉ CUBAN CUISINE
1998 CHERRY ROAD, ROCK HILL

"Feasting is also closely related to memory. We eat certain things in a particular way in order to remember who we are. Why else would you eat grits in Madison, New Jersey?"
Jeff Smith, 'The Frugal Gourmet Keeps the Feast'

SMOKED SALMON MILLEFEUILLE

Whether it's on one of the three Port Royal championship golf courses, our award-winning tennis courts, planning the perfect wedding or simply watching the day go by from a lounge chair by one of our pools-we offer endless ways to renew. Our Carolina Cafe is popular even with the locals for its variety and freshness!

5 oz. or 50 chips
1 seafood nacho set
(Lobster cream sauce,
salmon & southwest
shrimp)

Cheese sauce:
2 oz. American cheese
2 oz. heavy cream

Pinch chopped parsley

Seafood nacho set:
2 oz. lobster base
4 oz. heavy cream
3 oz. salmon pieces,
skin removed
3 oz. 31/40 shrimp
Cajun seasoning mix

Seafood Set:
1. Combine lobster base and heavy cream in a sauce pan over low heat. Cook, stirring constantly.

2. Add salmon, shrimp and Cajun seasoning mix (to taste). Cook until shrimp are done, about 5 minutes

Cheese Sauce:
1. Combine cheese and cream in a sauce pan over low heat until smooth.

Nachos:
1. Heat seafood nacho set in microwave for 2 minutes or until piping hot.

2. Place ½ of chips on plate and ladle 2 oz. cheese sauce over chips.

3. Add remaining chips and pour hot seafood set over cheese and chips.

4. Ladle remaining cheese sauce over seafood set.

5. Place dish under cheese melter until cheese is well browned. Sprinkle chopped parsley over entire dish.

Note: Cheese melter must be set on low heat in order to leave chips in long enough to heat thoroughly without burning.

WESTIN HILTON HEAD ISLAND RESORT, 2 GRASSLAWN AVENUE, HILTON HEAD

CAROLINA CAFE

"Carolina lowcountry is an almost irreversible antidote to the charms of other landscapes, other alien geographies. You can be moved profoundly by other vistas, by other oceans, by soaring mountain ranges, but you can never be seduced."
*Pat Conroy, **The Lords of Discipline***

KILLER DOG

Savor famous American cuisine at Carolina Roadhouse. Here you'll enjoy thick broiled steaks, "fall-off-the-bone" baby back ribs, giant seafood platters, the outrageous "Killer Dog" and award winning salads – all moderately priced. Displaying a wide-open show kitchen, large wrap-around bar featuring an extensive wine list and specialty cocktails – Carolina Roadhouse is a local's favorite and a "must visit" when in Myrtle Beach.

1 foot-long hot dog
1 foot-long bun
Gulden's Spicy Brown Mustard
12 oz. French fries
6 oz. chili
½ C. mixed cheese
1 Tbsp onions, chopped

1. Broil hot dog until hot and 25% charred.

2. Cook French fries until golden brown and crispy.

3. Place hot dog on bun.

4. Remove fries from fryer, season well, and cover hot dog with fries.

5. Ladle chili over fries.

6. Evenly spread cheese over chili and place in melter until cheese has completely melted.

7. Remove from melter and top with chopped onions.

Signature Tastes of SOUTH CAROLINA

CAROLINA ROADHOUSE
4617 N. KINDS HWY, MYRTLE BEACH

"Some people wanted champagne and caviar when they should have had beer and hot dogs."
Dwight D. Eisenhower, former President of the U.S.

WORLD FAMOUS "CRAB HOUSE" CRAB POT

"Family Owned for 20 years and Still Crackin", Charleston Crab House restaurants serve the best seafood and good times in Charleston. Open year-round, the Crab House serves lunch and dinner seven days a week. Both indoor and outdoor seating is offered and banquet rooms are available upon request for special occasions. Visit the Crab House on James Island for waterfront dining, Charleston's historic Market Street location for rooftop dining or the Mt. Pleasant location for patio dining. Reservations are recommended. Featuring: Snow Crab Legs, She Crab Soup, Lowcountry Shrimp Boil, Crab Cakes, Charleston Shrimp & Grits, Crispy Whole Flounder, Sesame Seared Tuna, Marinated Ribeye, Chicken Parmesan, Fresh Salads & Sandwiches, Kids menu & much more.

Scampi Butter:
3 large cloves garlic, peeled
1 green onion, chopped
2 Tbsp fresh parsley leaves
1 Tbsp lemon juice
½ C. unsalted butter, melted
Salt & pepper to taste

Crab Pot:
2 lbs snow crab legs, thawed
2 lbs Dungeness crab legs, thawed
2 lbs shrimp, 21/25 count, peeled & deveined
40 mussels
4 pieces fresh corn on the cob, shucked & cut in half
10 red skin potatoes, cut in half
2 yellow sweet onions. peeled & cut in half
1lb smoked sausage, cut in 2" pieces
Scampi butter
Cocktail sauce
Lemon wedges
Cocktail fork
Crab cracker

Scampi Butter:
1. In a mixing bowl, combine garlic, onion and parsley. Mix in lemon juice and butter until thoroughly combined. Season with salt & pepper. Use immediately or store in the refrigerator until ready to use.

Crab Pot:
1. In a large pot, steam potatoes, corn, sausage and onion for 10 minutes.
2. Add crab legs and cook for 3 minutes.
3. Add mussels and cook for 2 minutes. Everything should be submerged in boiling water – if not, add more hot water to cover.
4. Add shrimp and continue steaming for another 3-5 minutes.
5. Strain and place in serving dish. Pour scampi butter on top. Garnish with cocktail fork, lemon wedge and cocktail sauce. Oh and don't forget your Crab cracker!

Serves 4-6

"There was an Old Person of Hyde,
Who walked by the shore with his bride,
Till a Crab who came near,
fill'd their bosoms with fear,
And they said, 'Would we'd never left Hyde!'"
*Edward Lear, English artist, writer;
known for his 'literary nonsense' & limericks*

CHOCOLATE PEANUT BUTTER PRETZEL PIE

Chocolate Moose, founded by Kristin Cobb, is bringing great new tastes to Greenville. Enjoy simple and fresh desserts. Best of all – our desserts come in individual servings so you can mix and match and mmmmmmm! In developing "The Moose", Cobb went straight to dessert central, travelling to Capolona-Arezzo, Italy where she baked side-by-side with an Italian family. She learned Italian favorites like Tiramisu (known as Tira-moose Sue here!). This family-friendly cafe also features mile-high chocolate moose pie, hot chocolate, banana pudding and the founder favorite: cupcakes. After all, Kristin is known for her famous cupcakes, and Greenville will enjoy the same flavors that keep Charleston, Mount Pleasant and Columbia coming back for more.

Crust:
6 oz. Oreo cookie pieces, crushed into crumbs
2 oz. butter (1/2 stick), melted

Peanut Butter Filling:
2 C. peanut butter (we use natural organic)
2 8oz. blocks cream cheese, room temp
1 C. sugar
3 C. whipped cream

Chocolate Ganache:
2 C. chocolate chips
½ C. half & half

Topping:
Pretzels, crushed into large crumbs
Whipped cream
Mini Reese's cups
Whole pretzels (snaps or tiny twists)

Crust:
1. Place Oreo cookies in plastic bag and roll with rolling pin to crush.
2. Mix melted butter into the crumbs. Put about 1 to 1 ½ Tbsp of crumbs into the bottom of your individual cups. We use a 9 oz. squat cup. You can use also ramekins or custard cups.

Peanut Butter Filling:
1. In an electric mixer, beat together the peanut butter, cream cheese and sugar.
2. Fold in the whipped cream and mix on low until light and fluffy.
3. Add 1/3 C. of peanut butter mixture to each cup – on top of cookie crumbs.

Chocolate Ganache:
1. Heat the half & half until small bubbles form; do not boil.
2. Pour on top of chocolate chips and stir until chocolate is melted, smooth and creamy. Set aside to cool.

Topping:
1. Place 1 rounded Tbsp of pretzel crumbs on top of the peanut butter filling.
2. Place 1 ½ Tbsp of cooled chocolate ganache on top of pretzels.
3. Add some whipped cream and top with a ½ mini Reese's cup and a pretzel piece.
4. Chill for 30 minutes or more. Serve.

"All you need is love. But a little chocolate now and then doesn't hurt."
Charles M. Schulz

TRUFFLE SPOON BREAD

Signature Tastes of SOUTH CAROLINA

Chef Marc Collins draws inspiration from many cuisines around the world to create a menu that is truly unique to the Charleston restaurant scene. Drawing inspiration from historic Southern dishes and always highlighting what is local and in season, Chef Collins puts a healthful, distinctive spin on classic Lowcountry dishes. This means there is less butter and cream than typically found on Southern menus. Whole grains are incorporated to dishes and ingredients are used at the peak of flavor. The result is satisfying dishes that retain their bright, bold flavors without the large amounts of fat found in many restaurant dishes. From our Plantation Rice Bread Rolls made in house daily, to the selection of local seafood, to Pastry Chef Lovorn's incredible desserts, each dinner at Circa 1886 celebrates the region we call home.

Tomato Jelly:
10 Roma tomatoes, peeled
¾ C. sugar
1 large red bell pepper, roasted, seeded & peeled
¼ C. fresh orange juice
6 Tbsp lemon juice
3 cloves garlic, peeled
1 shallot
¼ tsp Tabasco
¼ tsp dried basil
Pinch crushed red pepper flakes

Parmesan Tuiles:
1 lb parmesan cheese, grated
1 large summer truffle, minced fine

Spoon Bread:
4 C. milk
1 Tbsp white truffle oil
1 C. cornmeal
2 Tbsp butter
1 ¾ tsp salt
White pepper to taste
4 eggs, separated
2 ½ C. cooked spaghetti squash, loosely packed
3 Tbsp summer truffle, minced
Fresh chives, minced
Micro mustard greens (available at The Chef's Garden)
Clarified butter

Tomato Jelly:
1. Place all ingredients into a saucepot, cooking over a moderate heat, stirring occasionally. Cook until everything is very soft and then pulse with a hand blender so that the mixture resembles jam. Cool and reserve for use.

Parmesan Tuiles:
1. Place the shredded parmesan in the shapes of triangles onto a silpat. Garnish with the minced truffles and bake in a convection oven at 350°F for 3-7 minutes. Keep a close eye on them; pull and cool completely.

Spoon Bread:
1. Cut spaghetti squash in half. Season with salt & white pepper and brush with clarified butter. Bake on a sheet tray, flesh side down, at 325°F convection oven for 20-35 minutes or until fork tender. Once cooked, "pull" and scrape out the flesh with a fork and set aside.
2. Lightly beat the egg yolks, set aside. Scald the milk and stir in the cornmeal. Cook this mixture for 3 minutes stirring constantly. Add the butter, truffle oil, salt and beaten egg yolks. Fold the spaghetti squash into the cornmeal mixture. Next whip the whites until light and fluffy and fold this into the cornmeal base. Add minced chives and truffles.
3. Place a ring mold atop a small cast iron pan and spoon mixture into it. Bake in a 350°F convection oven for 12-15 minutes. It should look like a firm soufflé when done.
4. Once cooked, run a knife around the ring mold and pull it off the spoon bread. Serve immediately garnished with the tomato jam spooned on top, then micro mustard greens and finally the parmesan tuile.

Wine: Pinot Gris, Westrey, Willamette Valley, Oregon 2001

149 WENTWORTH STREET, CHARLESTON

CIRCA 1886

"They can, on certain occasions, make women more tender and men more lovable."
Referring to truffles: Alexandre Dumas

SEARED PORK LOIN

In 2010, Chef Tray Mathis was fortunate enough to partner with SPACE (The Spartanburg Area Conservancy) to create the Food Group Farm. SPACE is a private, not-for-profit land conservation organization whose purpose is to protect and preserve natural areas of ecological, historical, and aesthetic value to enhance the quality of life for all residents and future generations in Spartanburg County. SPACE has opened their arms and generously allowed us to use the beautiful area, allowing for Chef Tray to participate in the cultivation and harvesting of his own products. The Food Group Farm is located just 10 miles from Converse Deli and will be producing a full crop this season sustaining both our restaurants with high quality local produce.

Pork Brine:
12 C. water
½ C. salt
½ C. sugar
12 peppercorns
6 cloves garlic
6 bay leaves

Goat Cheese Stuffing:
11 oz. goat cheese, room temp
¼ C. honey
1 C. pecans, chopped
1 tsp each fresh thyme, rosemary & basil
1 tsp each Celtic sea salt, toasted black pepper, onion powder, garlic powder, chipotle powder & brown sugar

Cider Reduction:
½ C. orange juice
2 C. local apple cider

Pork Loin:
Whole pork tenderloin
Extra virgin olive oil

Pork Brine:
1. Mix all ingredients and cook on stove top until all the salt and sugar has dissolved. Allow to cool to room temperature.

Goat Cheese Stuffing:
1. We use local goat cheese and local honey from the Bell family. Feel free to use your local favorites. Drizzle honey on the pecans then toast in the oven for a few minutes until golden brown.
2. Combine the goat cheese and the honey pecans in a food processor with the fresh front door garden herbs (thyme, rosemary, basil), Celtic sea salt, toasted black pepper, onion powder, garlic powder, chipotle powder and brown sugar. Reserve for use.

Cider Reduction:
1. Reduce the orange juice and apple cider by half, remembering to reserve some to be used to baste over the pork loin while cooking in the oven.

Pork Loin:
1. Portion the while pork loin into 3 sections and place in the pork brine. Refrigerate for up to 8 hours.
2. Using a kitchen (steal) create a hole through the middle pork loin section while rotating to make the hole big enough to insert the goat cheese stuffing.
3. Sear the stuffed pork loin in a pan on top and bottom and place on a cooking rack atop a lined sheet pan.
4. Place in oven and cook on low temperature for an hour or until reaching desired temperature. Make sure to alternate sides of pork while cooking.

To serve: slice the pork loin ¼" thick and bring to room temperature.

Signature Tastes of SOUTH CAROLINA

551 E. MAIN STREET SUITE 105, SPARTANBURG

CONVERSE DELI

"The fact is that it takes more than ingredients and technique to cook a good meal. A good cook puts something of himself into the preparation – he cooks with enjoyment, anticipation, spontaneity, and he is willing to experiment."
Pearl Bailey, 'Pearl's Kitchen'

Signature Tastes of SOUTH CAROLINA

To a Southerner, eating grits is practically a religion and breakfast without grits is unthinkable. A true grit lover would not consider instant or quick-cooking grits; only long-cooking stone ground grits are worth eating. In the Lowcountry of South Carolina, and particularly Charleston, shrimp & grits has been considered a basic breakfast for coastal fisherman and families for decades during the shrimp season. Simply called "breakfast shrimp", the dish consisted of a pot of grits with shrimp cooked in a little bacon grease or butter. During the past decade, this dish has been dressed up and taken out on the town to the fanciest restaurants. Not just for breakfast anymore – it's also served for brunch, lunch and dinner.

Grits:
1 qt. milk
1 C. stone ground grits
4 oz. unsalted butter, diced
1 C. heavy cream
1 C. sharp cheddar cheese, shredded

Shrimp:
2 lbs shrimp, peeled & deveined
¼ lb Andouille sausage, sliced
1 C. Tasso ham, shredded
1 shallot, minced
2 oz. white wine
2 C. chicken or vegetable stock
½ C. flour
2 oz. unsalted butter
1 scallion, thinly sliced
¼ qt. grape tomatoes, halved
2 Tbsp olive oil
Salt & pepper to taste

Grits:
1. Bring milk to boil in a heavy bottomed large pot. Slowly whisk in the grits.
2. Continue to stir over medium heat until the grits begin to thicken. Reduce the heat to low and continue to stir occasionally for approximately 20 minutes.
3. Slowly whisk in the cream and butter.
4. Bring to a simmer and stir in cheddar cheese. Season to taste.

Shrimp:
1. Bring the stock to a boil in a large pot.
2. Melt butter in saucepan and then slowly whisk the melted butter and flour to make a roux. Continue to stir over medium heat until golden brown.
3. Slowly whisk roux into stock over medium heat. Continue to simmer while stirring occasionally, until thick.
4. Heat a large pan over medium-high heat, then add oil.
5. Season the shrimp with salt & pepper and add to the pan. Spread shrimp evenly and cook for 30 seconds and then flip.
6. Add the shallots, sausage and ham. Stir gently and cook for 2 minutes.
7. Use the white wine to deglaze and add the chicken stock. Bring to simmer over medium heat and then season to taste.
8. Serve with the grits and garnish with sliced scallions and grape tomato halves.

1067 E. MONTAGUE AVENUE, N. CHARLESTON

CORK BISTRO

"An inexpensive, simple and thoroughly digestible food, [grits] should be made popular throughout the entire world. Given enough of it, the inhabitants of planet Earth would have nothing to fight about. A man full of [grits] is a man of peace."
The Charleston News and Courier, 1952

VEGGIE BURGER

Located in charming, historic downtown Conway, we're surrounded by unique shops, art galleries, theater life and the area's historic Riverwalk found on the Waccamaw River. We invite you to come in, relax and dine with us...whether you're a local or just visiting the area. Crady's serves an eclectic bistro menu in a retro European cafe-like setting. We're also known for our freshly prepared desserts and festive libations! Crady's estaurant & Bar is owned and operated by the Whitley family, with two generations currently working at the restaurant. We look forward to seeing you soon!

Veggie Burger:
3 C. water
2/3 C. Farro*
2/3 C. brown or green lentils
1/3 C. long grain brown rice
1/3 C. purple sticky rice
¼ C. vegetable oil
2 C. carrots, grated
1 C. onions, finely chopped
1 C. celery, finely chopped
¼ C. toasted sunflower kernel seeds
1 Tbsp garlic, minced
1 Tbsp chopped fresh basil or 1 tsp dried basil
2 Tbsp chopped fresh thyme or 2 tsp dried thyme
2 Tbsp chopped fresh oregano or 1 tsp dried oregano
2 Tbsp chopped fresh parsley or 1 tsp dried parsley
2 Tbsp chopped fresh cilantro or 1 tsp dried cilantro
4 eggs, beaten
3 ½ Tbsp all-purpose flour
Panko bread crumbs

Chipotle Mayonnaise:
½ C. low-fat mayo
1 Tbsp chipotle peppers (in adobo sauce), finely diced

*available in specialty foods section of market

1. Mix water, Farro, lentils and rice and cook until grains are soft. Let them cool.

2. Sauté carrots, onions, celery, sunflower kernels, and garlic in oil until tender.

3. Add herbs to the grains and vegetable mixture and then let cool.

4. Add eggs, flour and 5 Tbsp Panko bread crumbs. Mix well.

5. Shape into 4-6 oz. patties. Pat additional Panko bread crumbs onto patties.

6. Heat "film" of oil in frying pan, add patties and cook until golden brown.

7. Put each cooked patty onto a fairly substantial Kaiser roll (toasted) or inside a Pita.

8. If desired, place a slice of provolone cheese and melt on top of patty towards end of cooking.

9. Top with shredded lettuce, a slice of tomato and drizzle with chipotle mayonnaise.

CRADY'S RESTAURANT & BAR
332 MAIN STREET, CONWAY

"I am oppressed with a dread of living forever. That is the only disadvantage of vegetarianism."
George Bernard Shaw

Four Cheese Macaroni

Signature Tastes of SOUTH CAROLINA

2 qt. heavy cream, reduced in half
1 lb pasta (we use orecchiette)
1 ½ C. pepper jack cheese, hand grated
1 ½ C. aged cheddar cheese, hand grated
1 ½ C. fontina cheese, hand grated1
½ C. mozzarella cheese, hand grated
¼ C. olive oil
Salt & pepper to taste

1. Preheat oven to 375°F.

2. Reduce cream slowly in half in a medium size saucepan.

3. Cook the pasta in salted water al dente.

4. Cool down rapidly in cold water then drain all excess water. Coat the pasta lightly in olive oil to prevent sticking. Set aside.

5. Grate all the cheeses by hand keeping them separate. It's important to grate all the cheese by hand. Pre-bought grated cheese tends to have corn starch added to the cheese. This will change the texture of your final product.

6. When the cream is reduced, whisk in 1 C. of each of the cheeses, under a low heat until fully melted. Set aside off the heat.

7. Add together in a big mixing bowl the rest of the cheese, pasta and cheese sauce. Add salt & pepper to taste and mix very well without breaking up the pasta.

8. Add final ingredients to a casserole pan and bake at 375°F until lightly brown on top.

18 PINCKNEY STREET, CHARLESTON

CRU CAFÉ

"Life is a combination of magic and pasta."
Federico Fellini

HONEY & SOY GINGER SALMON WITH WASABI MASHED POTATOES

Delamater's Restaurant is located in what was originally the Bank of Newberry. Built in 1852, it was the first bank in SC west of Columbia. The interior of the dining room includes beautiful oak paneling and the original marble bank teller wall, as well as two of the three vaults the building houses. Located just three doors from the historic Newberry Opera House, Delamater's is one of only four structures in downtown Newberry that is listed on the National Register of Historic Places in South Carolina. We invite you to experience fine dining in a warm and casual atmosphere. Enjoy our varied American cuisine with an international flair.

Soy Ginger Reduction:
2 C. low sodium soy sauce
¾ C. honey
1 Tbsp fresh ginger, chopped

Wasabi Mashed Potatoes:
4 medium Yukon Gold potatoes
1 C. milk
1 tsp salt & pepper
4 Tbsp butter
1 Tbsp prepared Wasabi paste (reconstituted powder)

Salmon:
4 6 oz. salmon filets
¼ C. all-purpose flour
3 Tbsp olive oil
Salt & pepper to taste

Soy Ginger Reduction:
1. Combine soy sauce, honey, and ginger in a saucepan and cook over medium heat until reduced by half.
2. Strain ginger pieces out of sauce and then chill sauce.

Wasabi Mashed Potatoes:
1. Boil potatoes (with skin on) until tender when pierced with a fork.
2. Drain potatoes and mash, adding other ingredients until creamy.

Salmon:
1. Combine flour with salt & pepper in a bowl and dredge the salmon filets in the flour.
2. Heat olive oil in a sauté pan. Sauté salmon filets in the oil over medium heat until a slight crust forms on the outside of the salmon.
3. Place filets in a 350°F oven for about 5 minutes or until an internal temperature of 130°F is reached.
4. Place each salmon filet on a serving of wasabi mashed potatoes and drizzle with soy ginger reduction. Serve with vegetable of choice. (We serve asparagus spears).

Signature Tastes of SOUTH CAROLINA

DELAMATER'S RESTAURANT
1117 BOYCE STREET, NEWBERRY

"Only two things in this world are too serious to be jested on – potatoes and matrimony."
Irish saying.

Heirloom Tomato Gazpacho

Devereaux's, housed in a century-old cigar factory that's been transformed into a first-rate restaurant, is quickly becoming one of the most recognized culinary establishments in the South. Our contemporary American menu features French, Asian and Southern-influenced dishes that are often described as culinary masterpieces. Our highly acclaimed Chef's Tasting Menu and our Chef's Ultimate Tasting Menu consist of 5 to 10 courses, respectively, of the Chef's personal selections for the evening. This is our most requested style of menu and it allows each guest to experience multiple dishes and the true culinary expertise for which Devereaux's is renowned. The culinary team works in an open-air kitchen, allowing our guests to get a front row seat to the culinary magic.

8 heirloom tomatoes
1 cucumber
1 clove garlic
1 yellow bell pepper
3 stalks celery
¼ red onion
1 C. picked cilantro leafs
½ C. sherry vinegar
Salt to taste

1. Remove core from tomatoes. Peel the red onion and cut into quarters. Remove seeds from the yellow peppers.

2. Roughly chop the first 6 ingredients into ½" pieces and place in a food processor with a pinch of salt, vinegar and cilantro leaves.

3. Pulse until mixture is blended. Do not completely puree- make sure there are still small pieces of all vegetables.

4. Line strainer with double layer of cheese cloth and pour mixture in. Let drip overnight in refrigerator.

5. Reserve liquid, discard vegetables and season with salt to taste.

25 E. Court Street, Greenville

Devereaux's

Wikipedia: Gazpacho is a cold Spanish tomato-based raw vegetable soup, originating in the southern region of Andalucía. Gazpacho is widely consumed throughout Spain, neighboring Portugal (where it is known as gaspacho) and parts of Latin America. Gazpacho is mostly consumed during the summer months, due to its refreshing qualities and cold serving temperature.

VEAL MILANESE WITH MASCARPONE & FENNEL

Signature Tastes of SOUTH CAROLINA

Dianne's on Devine has been pioneering the fine dining industry in Columbia since 1995. Our exquisite Italian influenced cuisine, unmatched service and upscale ambiance have merited us such awards as: Best Wait Staff, Most Romantic and Best Fine Dining Restaurant. Expect a relaxing evening surrounded by a warm rich décor and dim lights as jazz softly plays in the background. Don't forget to visit our inviting lounge area where distinguished guests and professional bar keeps are sure to spark an interesting conversation.

Veal Milanese:
½ C. flour
3 large eggs, beaten
2 C. Italian seasoned bread crumbs
4-6 veal cutlets
1 C. olive oil
¼ C. butter

Sauce:
2 Tbsp butter
3 fresh Fennel stalks, trimmed & sliced thin
4 C. grape tomatoes
1 tsp fresh thyme
1 C. mascarpone cheese
Anise flavored liqueur to taste
Salt & pepper to taste

Veal Milanese:
1. Dredge each cutlet in flour, dip into egg wash, dredge in seasoned bread crumbs and set aside.
2. In large skillet, heat olive oil and butter over medium heat. Add the cutlets and cook on both sides until lightly golden brown.
3. Set cutlets aside on paper towels to absorb excess oil.

Sauce:
1. In large saucepan, melt butter over medium-high heat. Add fresh fennel and cook until transparent.
2. Combine grape tomatoes, mascarpone cheese, fresh thyme and salt & pepper into mixture until well blended.
3. Splash in Anise flavored liqueur to taste. Chef Prato uses Sambucca (anise flavored Italian liqueur) to replace some of the flavor that fresh Fennel loses during the cooking process.
4. Spoon over the Veal Milanese and your favorite cooked pasta.

Serves 4-6.

DIANNE'S ON DEVINE
2400 DEVINE STREET, COLUMBIA

"Veal is the quintessential Lonely Guy meat. There's something pale and lonely about it, especially if it doesn't have any veins. It's so wan and Kierkegaardian you just know it's not going to hurt you."
Bruce Jay Friedman, 'The Lonely Guy Cookbook'

Signature Tastes of SOUTH CAROLINA

Brother and sister duo, Bill Dunleavy & Patti Maher opened the doors of Dunleavey's Pub on April 15, 1992. We remain a family-owned and operated Pub, with Patti's son, Jamie Maher, joining the business in 1997. We host the annual Polar Bear Plunge benefitting the SC Special Olympics during which thousands of participants enter the chilly Atlantic on January 1st. Serving Shepherd's Pie, P.E.I. Mussels, Shrimp Burgers, Reubens Cheeseburgers, along with two homemade soups of the day. We'll be celebrating 20 years on April 15, 2012. We hope you stop by and celebrate with us!

2 cans lump crab meat
½ C. sour cream
½ C. mayo
½ C. ketchup
1 ½ C. cheddar and Monterey jack cheese mix
½ tsp garlic, chopped
Cayenne pepper to taste

1. Drain crab meat and remove any bits of cartilage. Break into small pieces.

2. Blend sour cream, mayo, ketchup, cheese blend and garlic until smooth.

3. Add crab and mix well. Season with cayenne pepper according to taste.

4. Chill several hours.

5. Serve with chips or crackers of your choice.

2213 MIDDLE STREET, SULLIVANS ISLAND

DUNLEAVY'S PUB

"The water temperature doesn't matter. It's the air and the wind. That's what you feel when you come up out of the water."
Bill Dunleavy, talking about the annual Polar Bear Plunge

WATERMELON & ARUGULA SUMMER SALAD

In 2005, Ricky Hacker and Matt McIntosh wheeled a cart into the Charleston Farmer's Market, built a fire and assembled an array of ingredients: handmade dough, homemade sauce, hand-pulled mozzarella and the freshest local produce. The result seemed simple enough – Extra Virgin Oven: fresh, honest, uncomplicated Neapolitan pizza. The line in front of the pizza cart grew longer…and longer. What was happening was delicious and different. Three years later, the cart still makes appearances – at private parties and gatherings. Now, the line forms inside Extra Virgin Oven's permanent location, in the heart of Historic Park Circle in North Charleston. In addition to pizza, Extra Virgin Oven serves an array of homemade soups, salads, cured meats and paninis on artisan breads, fresh from our wood-fired oven. Artisan beers on tap and distinctive European wines are the perfect complement to our honest food.

Signature Tastes of SOUTH CAROLINA

Pickled Red Onion:
1 medium red onion, sliced
½ C. white vinegar
½ C. water
3 Tbsp sugar
1 Tbsp pickling spice

Watermelon & Arugula Summer Salad:
5 lb watermelon, seeded & cubed
1 C. mint, roughly chopped
1 lb arugula
½ C. Mindoro bleu cheese, crumbled
1 pickled red onion, sliced
½ C. pine nuts, toasted
2 oz. raspberry vinegar
2 oz. extra virgin olive oil
Sea salt & cracked pepper to taste

Pickled Red Onion:
1. Combine vinegar, water, sugar and pickling spice in a pot. Bring to a boil. Stir then pour over onions. Chill for at least 1 hour before serving.

Watermelon & Arugula Summer Salad:
1. In a large mixing bowl, add arugula and mint. Season with salt & pepper.

2. Add bleu cheese, pickled onions and 3 Tbsp of the pine nuts.

3. Add raspberry vinegar and extra virgin olive oil. Toss lightly.

4. Place 6 cubes of watermelon on each salad plate. Add sea salt. Place one hand full of arugula mix on top of melon. Finish with remaining pine nuts and serve.

Makes 5 servings

EXTRA VIRGIN OVEN (EVO)
1075 E. MONTAGUE AVENUE, N. CHARLESTON

"The true Southern watermelon is a boon apart, and not to be mentioned with commoner things. It is chief of this world's luxuries, king by the grace of God over all the fruits of the earth. When one has tasted it, he knows what the angels eat. It was not a Southern watermelon that Eve took; we know it because she repented."
Mark Twain

LOBSTER MACARONI & CHEESE

Step through the revolving door and into a swanky restaurant with all the style of the Rat Pack era. Big booths, soft lighting and snappy service will take you back to the big city lounges of Chicago, Las Vegas and New York of the 50's and 60's. The huge Italian-American menu has something for everyone. Hand cut steaks, bone-inn chops, fresh seafood, pastas, flatbread pizzas and house made desserts.

1 1½ lb live lobster
¼ lb dry rigatoni pasta
½ stick butter
4 oz. half & half
4 oz. heavy cream
¼ C. parmesan cheese, finely grated
¼ C. Swiss cheese, shredded
¼ C. provolone cheese, shredded
¼ C. Italian fontina cheese, shredded*
2 tsp fresh thyme leaf
Salt to taste
¼ C. fine bread crumbs

1. Bring 2 pots of water to a boil.
2. In one pot, add salt and the whole lobster. Boil the lobster about 7 minutes.
3. Remove the lobster from pot and immediately shock in an ice bath.
4. After the lobster has cooled, remove the meat from the tail and claws and roughly chop. Reserve the head and tail for garnish. It's best to prepare the lobster ahead of time for this dish.
5. In the second pot, add salt and rigatoni. Cook until al dente, about 12 minutes.
6. In a heavy bottom, non-stick skillet, melt the butter and then add cream and half & half. Bring to a simmer for about 2 minutes.
7. Add the roughly chopped lobster meat, cooked rigatoni and 4 cheese blend. Stir and simmer for about 3 minutes on medium heat until all cheese is incorporated.
8. Fold in the fresh thyme leaf and then transfer the lobster/pasta to a 10" round pasta bowl.
9. Dust the top of the pasta with bread crumbs and bake in the oven at 350°F for about 5 minutes.
10. Garnish the pasta with the lobster head, tail and 2 sprigs of fresh thyme.

*Use Italian fontina as many other fontina cheeses tend to be younger, softer and blander.

FABULOUS FRANKIE BONES
1301 MAIN STREET, HILTON HEAD ISLAND

"I remember a time we called Camelot. It was the early 60's. A carefree time...a great time in America. The Rat Pack ruled and "swanky" and "high roller" meant a great show, great laughs and a great martini. My pals and my best gal travelled to the big casino cities and ate at all the best joints. Subway floors, leather booths and blacked out windows. Now that's culture. We celebrated big food, big wine, hand shaken martinis and...the simple things in life."
Frankie Bones

Welcome To

Fat Harold's
Beach
Club

Fat Harold's Famous Bologna Sandwich

The Fat Man, as he's affectionately called, came up with this sandwich when he opened The Shag City Grill which is located just inside the door of The World Famous Fat Harold's Beach Club! Shaggers, tourists, locals and even the neighborhood pets come by to get a Famous Bologna Sandwich at some point in time. Our staff, called The Fun Team would love to have you visit us and dive into one of our signature sandwiches. You won't be sorry you did! While here, you'll have to shag a little, sip on a cold libation, buy a t-shirt, or just browse through the years of memorabilia that lines the walls of Fat Harold's.

½″ thick bologna slice, hand cut
Corn-Dusted Bun
Favorite sandwich dressings

1. Throw the bologna slice on the grill to blacken to perfection, unless you prefer it rare (raw) or medium (grill marks only).

2. While the bologna is on the grill, steam a Corn-Dusted Bun and dress it starting with mayo, then adding lettuce, tomatoes, sliced onions, topped with the Bologna and mustard.

3. Serve with your choice of chips, crinkle fries or sweet tater fries.

Signature Tastes of SOUTH CAROLINA

FAT HAROLD'S BEACH CLUB
212 MAIN STREET, N. MYRTLE BEACH

"You Ain't Been To The Beach, Until You've Been To Fat Harold's Beach Club"!
The Fat Man

87

Shrimp & Crab Hoppin' John

Located on Johns Island, minutes from downtown Charleston, Fat Hen Restaurant pays homage to the Huguenot culture in Charleston by serving comfort food with a Lowcountry and French flair. Fat Hen's main dishes center around innovative French classics with Lowcountry flourishes. Our wine list features a grand variety of wines from around the world, showcasing the growing number of small sophisticated wineries. With a focus on fresh, local, delicious food, sensuous wines, comfortable design and warm hospitality, Fat Hen provides diners with a feast for the senses.

Beans:
2 C. dried black eyed peas
1 ham hock
4 C. water

Rice:
1 C. long-grain rice
1 medium yellow onion, diced
7 strips apple wood smoked bacon, diced
2 Tbsp sweet butter
½ C. green onion, minced
2 Tbsp lemon juice
Hot Sauce
Salt & pepper to taste

Shrimp & Crab:
1 tsp olive oil
2 oz. white wine
3 oz. chicken stock
¼ oz. zucchini, julienned
¼ oz. squash, julienned
¼ oz. carrot, julienned
1 oz. garlic butter
50 shrimp, peeled & deveined
2 oz. jumbo lump crab meat

Beans:
1. Rinse beans and place in a medium sauce pot and cover with water.
2. Add ham hock and bring to a boil and cook until tender (to speed up cooking time, soak beans overnight). When beans are tender, strain and cool. Reserve ham hock.
3. When cooled, pick meat off of ham hock and add back to the beans.

Rice:
1. Render the bacon and sweat the onion until tender. Add butter and melt.
2. Add rice and cook for 30 seconds. Cover rice with water (about 1 inch). Cook until all liquid is gone and rice is tender. Spread the rice mixture on a sheet tray and cool.
3. Mix rice, beans and green onion together. Season with hot sauce, salt, pepper and lemon juice. Remember, the mixture is cold, so do not over season. When the dish is heated back up, the flavors will awaken.

Shrimp & Crab:
1. In a sauté pan, add olive oil and heat to smoking point. Add shrimp, sauté on both sides just to color, then remove from pan.
2. Deglaze pan with white wine. Add vegetables, hoppin' john and chicken stock.
3. Add shrimp back to the pan along with the crab meat.
4. Finish with garlic butter and season with salt & pepper.
5. Check seasoning. Place on your favorite serving platter and garnish with chopped parsley. Makes 10 servings.

3140 Maybank Highway, Johns Island

Fat Hen

"I'm good in the kitchen. I can cook seafood, collard greens and black-eyed peas."
Monique Coleman, Actress

PEACH COBBLER

Welcome to a place that feels like home. Sure, other restaurants claim to be home grown or have a hometown appeal, but at FATZ, we really are "homemade." When you step into a FATZ, you'll feel special and you'll be treated like family. That's our mission. It always has been. FATZ was born in 1988 and was setup to serve the community, not some corporate bottom line. Our restaurants are run by folks who are part of their communities and who have a vested interest in serving you, our guests. If something isn't right, we'll make it right. We want to take care of you. After all that's what family members do for one another. So again, welcome to a place that feels like home. Welcome to FATZ!

Signature Tastes of SOUTH CAROLINA

Cobbler:
5 lbs peaches
1 C. cornstarch
1 ½ C. cold water
¼ C. peach brandy
1 qt. brown sugar, packed
1 tsp salt
2 tsp cinnamon
1 tsp nutmeg
3 sheets cobbler dough sheets

Topping:
1 ½ qt. walnuts, chopped to ½" x ½"
1 lb margarine
3 C. light brown sugar

Cobbler:
1. Line a full size hotel pan with the cobbler dough sheets making sure to seal all seams. Bake at 350°F for 10 minutes until golden brown.
2. In a large saucepan, mix cornstarch and cold water, stirring until smooth.
3. Combine peach brandy to cornstarch mixture, over medium heat and bring to a boil while stirring constantly. Continue boiling until mixture is thick and clear.
4. Add brown sugar, salt, cinnamon and nutmeg to the mixture and remove from heat.
5. Fold in peaches and cool thoroughly.
6. Pour peach mixture into crust and then cover with additional crust, being sure to seal the edges.
7. Bake at 275°F for 45 minutes. Crust should be golden brown.

Topping:
1. Chop the walnuts until they are the desired size (½" x ½").
2. In a small saucepan, combine the butter and brown sugar. Place on low heat. Stir constantly until mixture becomes caramel like. It should be smooth with no hint of sugar granules. Do not boil.
3. Remove from heat and fold in walnut pieces.
4. Pour mixture evenly over the top crust of the cobbler.
5. Place back in the oven at 275°F for 20 minutes.
6. Remove and cool before cutting.

MULTIPLE LOCATIONS ACROSS THE STATE

FATZ CAFÉ

"Chocolate's okay, but I prefer a really intense fruit taste. You know when a peach is absolutely perfect... it's sublime. I'd like to capture that and then use it in a dessert."
Kathy Mattea, Musician

BBQ COLLARDS

Fiery Ron's Home Team BBQ prepares Charleston's best BBQ and ribs with traditional methods and processes. Using only fresh ingredients, our salads, tacos, sandwiches and wraps are created with a unique approach to BBQ. Our dry rubbed ribs, chicken and pork shoulders combined with finger lickin' sides will knock your socks off! We offer takeout orders, catering and delivery. Home Team BBQ has something for everyone with award-winning food and a rockin' bar with weekly live music and sports on the TV's. Come for a work lunch, casual family dinner or a fun night out with friends.

1 gallon water
3 C. cider vinegar
¼ C. hot sauce
½ C. brown sugar
½ C. kosher salt
2 to 3 shoulder bones or smoked ham hocks
½ lb smoked pork shoulder, chopped or pulled
2 lbs collard greens, cut in 2" strips

1. Bring water to a simmer.

2. Add cider vinegar, hot sauce, brown sugar and kosher salt.

3. Add bones or ham hocks for flavor and simmer for 25 minutes.

4. Add greens and smoked pork.

5. Simmer lightly for 2-3 hours or until tender.

FIERY RON'S HOME TEAM BBQ
WEST ASHLEY - SULLIVAN'S ISLAND

"Part of the secret of success in life is to eat what you like and let the food fight it out inside."
Mark Twain

SCALLOPS WITH ROASTED SPAGHETTI SQUASH & BACON CARAMEL

A unique restaurant in a unique neighborhood. Fish Market is York county's premier destination for the finest fresh seafood available in a comfortable, warm setting by a team of knowledgeable and attentive staff. The Chef's signature menu features a wide selection of seafood, inspired by fresh local produce and high quality ingredients. We also offer live Maine lobsters, chicken and steak, and a daily selection of desserts made in house. Conveniently located off interstate I-77 in Fort Mill's Baxter Village, Fish Market Seafood, Bar & Grill is just a short drive for residents of Charlotte, NC and Rock Hill, SC.

6 large sea scallops
6 strips good quality smoked bacon
1 large spaghetti squash
½ C. sugar
¼ C. water
1 tsp heavy cream
Salt & pepper to taste

1. Cut squash in half and remove seeds.

2. Season liberally with salt & pepper and roast in a 350°F oven for 45 minutes or until soft and the flesh is easily pulled from the skin.

3. Discard the skin of the squash. Break up the strands of tender spaghetti squash to serve along with scallops.

4. Dice the bacon and render in a small pot until browned.

5. Incorporate sugar and water with a whisk. Bring to a boil, then add cream and reduce heat to simmer for about 5 minutes. Strain and discard the bacon.

6. Season the scallops to taste with salt & pepper. Sear in a hot pan with canola or your choice of vegetable oil.

7. Serve the scallops and squash with a drizzle of bacon caramel.

Signature Tastes of SOUTH CAROLINA

FISH MARKET SEAFOOD, BAR & GRILL
990 MARKET STREET, FORT MILL

"Life expectancy would grow by leaps and bounds if green vegetables smelled as good as bacon."
Doug Larson

FISH SPECIALTIES
Menu:
Fish specialties, seafood, fish soup
Carp, perch, pike, salmon, tuna
RESTAURANT

A warm, eclectic and inviting space, Fish Restaurant resides in a beautifully renovated, 1837 Charleston home in the heart of the Upper King Design District. Fish showcases the finest local, sustainable ingredients with an always-changing menu and a French-Asian flair. Executive Chef Nico Romo, the youngest chef to ever earn the distinction of Master Chef of France, blends his skills at creating classic French fare with a zesty Asian-inspired artisan touch, resulting in fresh and flavorful dishes that engage and inspire. Chef Romo and our passionate team work closely with local fishermen and farmers to source the freshest, most flavorful ingredients that bring our culinary creations to life.

Broth:
1 can (14 oz.) coconut milk
1 celery stalk, chopped
½ onion, diced
¼ C. ginger, chopped
¼ C. garlic, chopped
½ C. white wine
2 tsp salt
1 kaffir lime leaf
1 lime, juiced
¼ tsp freshly ground black pepper
½ piece of lemon grass, chopped
A couple fish bones

Fish:
3 or more different kinds of local fish cut into small pieces (4 oz. porgy, scallops, shrimp)
4 clams
½ C. olive oil
½ C. shallots, thinly sliced
½ garlic clove, crushed

Vegetables:
1 fingerling potato
1 leaf baby bok choy
3 oyster mushrooms
¼ sweet red pepper, sliced
¼ tsp freshly ground black pepper
2/3 C. white wine
Sliced French baguette bread

Broth:
1. Combine all ingredients together in a large pot and simmer for 25 minutes.
2. Skim the broth and pass through chinois.

Fish & Vegetables:
1. Heat ¼ cup of olive oil in a large (6 qt.) saucepan.
2. Sear the scallops, fish and shrimp and then remove from the pan.
3. In the same pan, drop the clams, garlic and shallots, add broth and bring to a boil.
4. Once boiling, add all the vegetables to the pan and sauté until the vegetables are crunchy and clams cooked thoroughly.
5. Add crushed garlic (more or less to taste), fresh ground pepper and sweet red pepper.
6. Salt & pepper to taste and lime juice if needed.

To serve: Place a thick slice of crusty French bread into a soup bowl, plain or lightly toasted. Spoon the vegetable, fish and broth mixture over the bread and enjoy.

FISH RESTAURANT
442 KING STREET, CHARLESTON

"What will be the death of me are buillabaisses, food spiced with pimiento, shellfish, and a load of exquisite rubbish which I eat in disproportionate quantities."
Emile Zola, French writer

SHRIMP & GRITS

Flying Fish Public Market & Grill features an assorted mix of local seafood, Lowcountry recipes and a raw bar with a wide variety of steamed shellfish, sushi, as well as smoked fish dips and homemade soups. We offer guests an additional and unique option for great casual dining on the water. We also offer a great selection of fresh fish, a wide variety of shellfish including shrimp, crab legs and oysters from our public seafood market. Enjoy the ocean's best offerings and get fresh seafood to go from the Flying Fish Public Market today!

Signature Tastes of SOUTH CAROLINA

FLYING FISH PUBLIC MARKET & GRILL
4744 US 17 SOUTH, BAREFOOT LANDING, N. MYRTLE BEACH

Grits:
1 C. stone ground grits
2 ½ C. water
1 C. heavy cream
2 Tbsp unsalted butter
2 tsp salt
1 C. cheddar cheese, grated

Shrimp:
2 Tbsp olive oil
1 ½ lbs shrimp, peeled & deveined
½ C. country ham, diced
1 C. grape tomatoes, halved
2 ½ C. heavy cream
¼ C. green onion, sliced
Salt & pepper to taste

Grits:
1. In a medium saucepan, place the grits, water, cream, butter and salt. Stir until blended and bring to a boil. Reduce heat to medium and continue to stir until the grits get thick, approximately 40 minutes. When the grits are done they will be soft, not gritty. Fold in cheese.

Shrimp:
1. Place a large sauté pan on the stove and get it hot. Add olive oil, shrimp, ham and season with salt & pepper.
2. Sear the shrimp on both sides; remove from the pan and place on a plate lined with paper towels.
3. Add tomatoes and cook for 2 minutes. Add heavy cream and bring to a boil. Reduce heat and let simmer for 3-4 minutes or until it starts to thicken.
4. Add the shrimp back to the mixture to finish cooking. After 3 minutes, add the green onion and simmer for 2 more minutes.

To serve: Place the grits in 4 bowls, cover each with the shrimp sauce and enjoy.

"I love the food of the South, and shrimp and grits is about as Southern as you can get. Once you get past the amount of time it takes to cook real grits (don't use the instant stuff), it is a very easy dish to pull off and cleanup is easy as it only uses two pans. I have converted many Northerners and non-grits believers with this recipe."
Chef Eric Martines

CREAMY SHRIMP & GRITS

Grits:
1 C. water
1 C. half & half or whole milk
2 oz. butter
1 C. stone-ground grits
Salt & white pepper to taste

Gravy Charleston Shrimp:
6 strips of bacon, sliced into ¼" pieces
1 lb small shrimp, peeled & deveined
8 scallions, thinly sliced keeping green & white separate
2 medium tomatoes, peeled, seeded & diced
¼ C. flour
1 ½ C. half & half or milk
Salt & cayenne or white pepper to taste

1. In a small saucepan combine the water, milk and butter.
2. Add salt to taste (it's important to add the salt before the grits), bring to a simmer and add the grits.
3. Cook over medium-low heat for 10-15 minutes until grits are tender. Add white pepper to taste. Cooked grits should have the same consistency as oatmeal or cream of wheat.

Gravy Charleston Shrimp:
1. Cook bacon until crisp in a sauté pan.
2. Add shrimp and scallion whites to the pan and sauté until the shrimp just begins to firm up.
3. Dust the mixture with flour and stir until well blended.
4. Add tomatoes and half & half, stir until well blended.
5. Bring to a simmer, stirring occasionally. Season with salt & pepper.
6. Serve immediately over grits or rice and garnish with the remaining scallion greens. Excellent accompaniments are crisp bacon slices and fresh sliced beef steak tomatoes.

Serves 4.

Signature Tastes of SOUTH CAROLINA

FOUR MOONS RESTAURANT & BAR
1145 ORANGEBURG MALL CIRCLE, ORANGEBURG

"I come from a home where gravy is a beverage."
Erma Bombeck, Journalist

Pan Fried Cornmeal & Black Pepper Encrusted Grouper

Signature Tastes of SOUTH CAROLINA

Grouper:
4 6 oz. pieces boneless skinless grouper
1 C. unbleached all-purpose flour
1 C. milk
2 C. stone-ground cornmeal
½ C. coarsely cracked black pepper
Salt & pepper to taste

Grits:
1 C. grits
3 C. water
2 C. heavy cream
2 oz. butter
2 C. parmesan cheese, shredded
Salt & pepper to taste

Three Peppercorn Cream Sauce:
1 Tbsp butter
1 C. heavy whipping cream
½ C. dry vermouth
½ C. smooth Dijon mustard
2 shallots; minced
2 Tbsp dried pink peppercorns
2 Tbsp dried green peppercorns
1 Tbsp cracked black pepper
½ C. vine ripened tomato; diced & seeded
½ C. green onions, thinly sliced
Salt & pepper to taste

Grouper:
1. Pour the milk in a bowl. Add the grouper filets to the milk and refrigerate. In a second bowl, combine the cornmeal, flour, salt & pepper and set it aside while making the grits.
2. Once the grits have been prepared, preheat the oven to 450°F. Remove the grouper from the refrigerator and dip fish into flour mixture. Heat a large oven proof pan with ¼" of canola oil. Remove from flour and shake off excess flour. Add fish to pan and cook until nicely browned; about 2-3 minutes. Flip the fish and place in the preheated oven. Cook fish approximately 10 minutes (depending on the thickness of the fish). While the fish is cooking, prepare the sauce.

Grits:
1. Bring water and cream to a boil in a large saucepan; season with salt & pepper. Add grits and return to a boil. Reduce the heat to medium-low and cook; stirring often for about 30-45 minutes (adding more water if the grits become too thick). Cooked grits should have a smooth creamy texture with the consistency of thin mashed potatoes. When the grits are done, add the butter and cheese and mix well. Cover and keep warm.

Three Peppercorn Cream Sauce:
1. Heat butter in a saucepan. Add the shallots and cook about 1 minute. Add the vermouth and cook an additional minute. Add the cream, mustard and peppercorns and bring to a boil. Reduce the heat and simmer until the sauce has thickened slightly and season with salt. When the sauce has thickened even more; add the green onions and tomatoes. Cook an additional minute.

To serve: Remove the fish from the oven (it should flake apart easily). Place the fish on a paper towel lined plate and keep warm. Divide the grits between 4 serving plates. Place 1 piece of fish on top of the grits on each plate. Ladle the sauce over the fish and garnish with chopped parsley and serve.

FRANK'S & FRANK'S OUTBACK
10434 OCEAN HIGHWAY, PAWLEYS ISLAND

"The only kind of seafood I trust is the fish stick, a totally featureless fish that doesn't have eyeballs or fins."
Dave Barry, 'Miami Herald' Columnist

ZUCCHINI CAKES WITH COOKED TOMATO COULIS

Overlooking Lake Hartwell, Friends at the Cove provides the perfect casual fine dining experience. We emphasize using the freshest and best local ingredients available to prepare fun and exciting nightly Chef's specials as well as our staple menu items. The restaurant settings are beautiful; the possibilities are endless. We provide that unique dining experience you've been looking for, accompanied by culinary masterpieces you've grown to love. You invite the guests and we'll do the rest.

Signature Tastes of SOUTH CAROLINA

Zucchini Cakes:
4 C. zucchini, grated
¼ C. carrots, grated
Dash Texas Pete
2 cloves garlic, chopped
Pinch of mixed Italian seasoning
1 sleeve saltine crackers, crushed
1-2 C. rice, cooled
2-4 Tbsp mayo

Cooked Tomato Coulis:
5 Tbsp olive oil
- C. shallots, finely chopped
3 cloves garlic, crushed
2 lbs plum tomatoes, quartered
Bouquet garnis made with thyme, rosemary, bay leaf & a lemon twist
1 tsp sugar or honey (optional)
2 Tbsp chopped basil, mint oregano or parsley (optional)
Salt & pepper to taste

Zucchini Cakes:
1. Grate zucchini and carrots. Add garlic, Texas Pete and seasonings; mix well. Add rice and part of the saltines and mix. Add enough mayo to bind. Adjust cracker and mayo proportions as necessary to make mixture that will hold together. Salt & pepper to taste and refrigerate for an hour if possible.
2. Spray bottom of a non stick pan, place scoop of mix in pan and flatten. Sauté until golden brown. Top with cooked tomato coulis and serve.

Cooked Tomato Coulis:
1. Heat oil in sauté pan. Add shallots, garlic and sauté until translucent, about 5 minutes. Add tomatoes and garnis and simmer over low heat till all the moisture is gone. Add sugar or honey if using.
2. Remove garnis and transfer sauce to a food processor and process until smooth. Pour sauce in a clean pan, bring to a boil, then remove from heat and season to taste. Add herbs if using. Serve over zucchini cakes or any other meat or fish. Shelf life is 1 week in refrigerator, 3 months in freezer.

FRIENDS AT THE COVE
1500 PROVIDENCE CHURCH ROAD, ANDERSON

The mission of the business from the beginning has been "serve the freshest ingredients possible, be thankful for all your bounty, and be good stewards to all that comes your way".
Valerie Lowe & Katie Tillman

Gambas al Ajillo (Spanish Shrimp with Garlic)

Located in the beautiful Congaree Vista, Gervais & Vine is a Spanish-styled tapas bar with culinary influences from all across the Mediterranean. In addition to over 40 wines by-the-glass, we offer a wide selection of craft beers and top-shelf spirits. As our guests, you're free to enjoy a small bite or load your table with many different tapas to share without ever running out of choices. We hold wine tastings, winemaker dinners and many other special events that revolve around food, drink and fun. This is our version of a classic Spanish tapas bar staple. It can be served on individual plates, but we like it best when it's served in the pan and everyone gathers around to enjoy in true tapas style.

1 lb shrimp 31/40, peeled & deveined
1 Tbsp chili powder
1 Tbsp paprika
½ tsp cayenne pepper
1 tsp salt
3 Tbsp olive oil
2 Tbsp garlic, minced
½ C. tomato, diced
3 slices bacon, broken into bits
1 C. dry sherry
3 Tbsp butter
Salt to taste
Lemon wedges
Chopped parsley
Toasted slices of rustic bread

1. In a sauté pan over medium-high heat, add olive oil.

2. When hot, add shrimp and seasonings, and sauté until they are cooked halfway.

3. Add garlic, tomatoes and bacon and sauté a bit longer.

4. Add sherry and cook until reduced by half.

5. Add butter and stir in. Season to taste with salt, if necessary.

6. Sprinkle with parsley and squeeze the lemon wedges over the shrimp. Serve with crusty bread.

GERVAIS & VINE
620-A GERVAIS STREET, COLUMBIA

"Tapas are Spain's greatest food invention. 'Eat when you drink, drink when you eat' is the philosophy. Spanish men traditionally drink outside the home and rarely alone. They are not meant to be a meal. One tapa per person and a different one with each drink is the idea, then everyone enjoys tasting and sharing. Tapas food is real food - good local ingredients presented with flair."
Tapa Recipes

Signature Taste of SOUTH CAROLINA

There's just something about fried chicken that reaches out across all ages and cultures. At the GO, we serve it only on Tuesday nights, and this is truly a special occasion. We believe that ours is extra special because we use all-natural chickens. These days it's not overly difficult or expensive to find such birds, and we swear you can taste the difference! Don't be intimidated by this recipe – just allow yourself time to brine and time to fry. The good thing about fried chicken is that it tastes really good at room temperature. So unlike fried seafood, you could do all the work in advance and sit down to enjoy the feast with your friends/family without forsaking flavor!

Buttermilk Brined Chicken:
1 qt. buttermilk
¼ C. hot sauce
¼ C. kosher salt
2 tsp garlic, minced
2 tsp freshly ground black pepper
1 tsp cayenne pepper
1 whole chicken (3 ½ to 4 pounds) cut into 8 serving pieces

Buttermilk Fried Chicken:
Vegetable oil for frying
1 buttermilk-brined chicken
2 C. self-rising flour
2 C. all-purpose flour
1 ½ Tbsp kosher salt
1 Tbsp freshly ground black pepper
1 Tbsp freshly ground white pepper
1 tsp cayenne

Buttermilk Brined Chicken:
1. Combine buttermilk, hot sauce, salt, garlic, pepper, and cayenne in a large bowl; stir to combine. Add chicken and make sure all pieces are submerged. Cover and refrigerate for 24 hours.

Buttermilk Fried Chicken:
1. Heat 4" of oil to 325°F in a large pot. Combine self-rising flour, all-purpose flour, salt, black pepper, white pepper, and cayenne in a brown paper grocery bag. Two bags – one inside the other – ensures no blowouts!
2. Remove chicken from the buttermilk and shake to remove excess. Add the chicken in batches to the flour mixture (in the bag) and shake to completely coat. Remove and shake over trash can to remove excess flour. Alternatively, you could simply combine the flour/seasoning in a shallow baking dish and dredge the chicken pieces through it. However, the paper bag method thoroughly coats the chicken and, in our opinion, happens to be more fun!
3. Place on a wire rack set over a baking sheet to rest until ready to fry, at least 30 minutes. Allowing the chicken to rest after flouring ensures that the flour will better adhere to the chicken during the frying process.
4. Fry the chicken in batches, skin-side down, until golden brown, about 8 minutes. Turn and fry until golden brown on the second side and cooked through, about 8 minutes longer. Remove and drain on paper towel-lined sheet pan. An instant-read thermometer should read 165°F when chicken is probed. If your chicken happens to be slightly under, you can finish it in the oven at 350°F. Note: An even oil temperature is key to frying at home. A clip-on candy/fry thermometer should be kept in the pot at all times, and the temperature should register at least 300°F during the frying process. Makes 4 to 6 servings.

GLASS ONION
1219 SAVANNAH HWY, CHARLESTON

"One of the delights of life is eating with friends, second to that is talking about eating. And, for an unsurpassed double whammy, there is talking about eating while you are eating with friends."
Laurie Colwin 'Home Cooking'

SZECHUAN CHICKEN SALAD

Signature Tastes of SOUTH CAROLINA

Nimrata Nikki Randhawa Haley (Born on January 20, 1972), an American politician, is the 116th and current Governor of South Carolina. A member of the Republican Party, Haley represented Lexington County in the South Carolina House of Representatives from 2005 to 2010. Haley is the first woman to serve as Governor of South Carolina, and the second Indian-American governor in the country. At the age of 40, Haley is the youngest current governor in the US. Haley signed a law cracking down on illegal immigration in June 2011. She also supports a law requiring photo identification at the polls.

2 qt. water
1 slice fresh ginger
1 green onion, split in half lengthwise
2 whole chicken breasts, about 2 lbs
¼ C. canola oil
1 tsp whole peppercorn
3 green onions, chopped
3 slices fresh ginger
3 cloves garlic, minced
½ tsp crushed red pepper flakes or Szechuan pepper
1 Tbsp honey
1 Tbsp Hoisin sauce
1 Tbsp soy sauce
1 head lettuce, shredded

1. In a pot, poach chicken for 15 minutes. Let stand in broth for 15 minutes and then remove the skin, bones and shred the meat.

2. In a small saucepan, heat oil. Crush peppercorns with mortar and pestle and add to oil along with the onion, ginger and garlic. Bring to a boil and boil 2 minutes.

3. Meanwhile, in a heatproof bowl, blend honey, Hoisin sauce and soy sauce. Pour in the hot oil mixture and stir to blend.

4. Turn shredded lettuce into a large bowl, add chicken and sauce. Serve and enjoy!

GOVERNOR NIKKI HALEY
800 RICHLAND STREET, COLUMBIA

"Agribusiness is such a vital part of our state's economy, contributing some $34 billion each year and employing more than 200,000 South Carolinians."
Governor Nikki Haley

LOUISIANA BEER-B-QUE SHRIMP

Heidi and Joe Trull each bring a life-long love of home cooking to their restaurant, Grits & Groceries. In addition to the regular menu of heaping servings of "real food, done real good," we offer daily specials that combine Cajun, Creole and Southern cooking traditions. Our world-class homemade dessert menu changes daily and Saturday brunch is an extravaganza of special dishes that make your mouth water just reading the menu! Grits & Groceries is a great place to meet and eat, and is included on the South Carolina National Heritage Corridor. Old friends and new are welcome at Grits & Groceries – just be sure to come hungry!

Signature Tastes of SOUTH CAROLINA

*5 lbs jumbo shrimp
1 Tbsp Low Country Seasoning**
1 C. Louisiana Beer-B-Que Sauce*
*½ lb butter
4 C. white mushrooms, halved
1 can beer, preferably malt liquor
¼ C. fresh parsley, finely chopped
Salt & pepper to taste*

1. Season shrimp with Low Country Seasoning.

2. Combine sauce and butter in a large sauté pan or saucepan over medium heat and cook until butter melts, stirring to combine.

3. Add the shrimp, mushrooms and beer, stir to combine and then cover.

4. Cook until shrimp are pink and firm, about 10 minutes. Season with salt & pepper.

5. Serve with grits, rice or mashed potatoes. Garnish with parsley.

Serves 8.

*Available at Grits & Groceries

GRITS & GROCERIES
2440 DUE WEST HIGHWAY, BELTON

"This is a play on the New Orleans dish of barbecue shrimp. I decided that we had to make it in a South Carolina Style – so, I started using my Carolina – inspired Beer-B-Que Sauce."
Heidi Trull

113

The History of the Groucho's® name is a story unto itself, and one that can only be told as follows. Harold "Groucho" Miller came to Columbia, South Carolina in 1941 with a handful of original recipes for potato salad, cole slaw, and various salad and sandwich dressings, most of which were thought up during his childhood in a Philadelphia orphanage. Throughout the generations, Groucho's Deli has held true to the idea of using only the highest quality products and ingredients, which has in turn led Groucho's® to a legendary status.

**(1) Pouch of Knorr Chili Base
(2) pints Chili Sauce
4oz. Roasted Garlic Pepper
1 (16 oz.)can Boned Chicken
1 bag of Simplot Veggie Mix (black bean/corn)
2oz. Chipotle Tabasco Sauce**

1. Combine the chili base, chili sauce and garlic pepper into a large stock pot over a medium heat.

2. Bring to a low simmer stirring to combine.

3. Add the chicken and veggie mix, stir to combine and then cover.

4. Cook for about 20 minutes, but not so much that the veggies get too soft.

5. Add the Tabasco toward the end and stir in.

Serves 8.

MULTIPLE LOCATIONS ACROSS THE STATE

GROUCHO'S

"When Pop first opened this store, Columbia was a small town, and everything had a label. Here he (Harold Miller) was this really crazy kind of guy. Always, joking. Always had a big cigar. A mustache. He looked like Groucho Marx, he talked like Groucho Marx, and to Columbia, he was Groucho Marx. So that is how the name came about."
Ivan Miller, in an interview with the Columbia Record

FRIED GREEN TOMATOES

Halls Chophouse is a family restaurant located in the Upper King District of Charleston. We value hospitality, superior American cuisine and a dining experience that guests revere. We present delicious cuisine in an energetic, visually striking environment featuring exposed brick walls, leather banquettes and warm lighting true to old-world traditional steakhouses. The 160-seat chophouse is situated on two rustic floors with tables and banquettes available for general dining. The first floor also offers a 16-seat antique African mahogany bar and a lounge, while a hardwood stairway to the second floor reveals a masterful 350-bottle wine rack, hallway bar and a private dining room. Complemented by superior service and a knowledgeable staff, Halls Chophouse offers sophisticated, quality cuisine.

1 lb apple wood smoked bacon, sliced
2 C. roasted corn, cut off cob
2 C. fresh tomatoes, diced
Olive oil
1 Tbsp blackening seasoning
1 C. heavy cream
½ lb lump crab meat & small shrimp
6 green tomatoes, sliced ¼" thick
1 C. buttermilk
1 C. cornmeal
2 C. all-purpose flour
2 Tbsp Old Bay
Salt & pepper to taste

1. In large saucepan, cook bacon, corn and tomatoes in a little olive oil over medium heat for 10 minutes.

2. Add blackening seasoning and heavy cream; simmer on low until reduced by half.

3. Stir in shrimp and crabmeat and add salt & pepper to taste.

4. Soak tomato slices in buttermilk.

5. Combine cornmeal, flour and Old Bay in bowl.

6. Dredge tomato slices in breading mixture and pan fry in olive oil until golden brown.

7. Top with shrimp and crab mixture.

HALLS CHOPHOUSE
434 KING STREET, CHARLESTON

"The food in the South is as important as food anywhere because it defines a person's culture."
Fannie Flagg, from the movie Fried Green Tomatoes

COLLARD GREENS

Joining Hamptons from the renowned Inn at Little Washington, Executive Chef Raffaele Dall'Erta is the quintessential epicure. Born and raised in Milan, Raffaele discovered the joy of cooking by the age of 5. Influences such as his father's love of cooking and visits to his grandparents in Parma fueled his passion for delicious food and broadened his culinary knowledge. These early experiences inspired Chef Dall'Erta to embark on a culinary career at age 15. Raffaele attended culinary school at Vallesana in Northern Lombardy, followed by apprenticeships which led to positions in top Italian kitchens including Don Lisander and La Rondine. In addition, Chef Dall'Erta has worked in such world-renowned restaurants as The Fat Duck in the United Kingdom and Per Se in New York. The combination of these culinary adventures have forged Raffaele's diverse menu. Raffaele looks forward to welcoming you to Hamptons and delivering a culinary experience you will never forget.

2 C. bacon, cut into small dices
2 bunches collard greens
1 onion, finely diced
3 shallots, minced
6 cloves garlic, minced
1 (6) pack beer (we use Charleston Lagerhead Lager)
½ C. Verjus (apple cider vinegar may be substituted)
1 tsp Old Bay
Salt to taste
Sugar to taste

1. Cook diced bacon until crispy in a large pot or Dutch oven on medium heat.

2. Add onion and allow to sweat for 2 minutes.

3. Add garlic and shallots and stir for an additional minute before adding the collard greens.

4. Deglaze pan using 1 beer (the rest are for you), reduce heat to medium-low and cook for 1 hour until greens are very tender and cooked through (all liquid has evaporated).

5. Add Verjus and season with remaining ingredients.

6. Collard greens should have a complex sweet-savory and tangy (from the Verjus) flavor. Keep warm, or re-warm if making in advance.

Signature Tastes of SOUTH CAROLINA

FOUR WEST HAMPTON AVENUE, SUMTER

HAMPTON'S

"I want to create good food that makes people happy."
Chef Raffaele Dall'Erta

119

Signature Tastes of SOUTH CAROLINA

We're the Hunter-Gatherer, a Columbia-based brew pub. We've been offering up traditional English-style ales since 1995. We brew them ourselves and we're the only place in the world you can get them. Besides the phenomenal beer, you'll also find a lot of other things to enjoy at the H-G, like a variety of fresh, home-made dishes we prepare right in our kitchen, a low-key atmosphere that's conducive to great conversation and plenty of interesting, diverse people. We're selective about our music, too. You'll hear a variety, from jazz to alternative and folk. Whether it's live music from a local group or selections from our extensive library, you'll find the sounds to be unique and comfortable. So come check us out. We're tucked away on South Main, right behind the capital building.

25-30 unopened mussels
2 shallots, minced
1 Tbsp garlic,
finely minced
2 stalks celery, minced
1 link dried,
cured Chorizo
2 C. IPA (Pale ale Beer)
1 Tbsp extra virgin
olive oil
1 Tbsp butter
Salt & pepper to taste

1. Wash and clean the mussels, discarding any opened ones.

2. Pour olive oil in a sauté pan and sweat the shallots, celery and Chorizo over medium-high heat for 2 minutes.

3. Add the mussels and after 2 minutes, add the garlic. Sauté for an additional 2 minutes.

4. Add beer and butter. Cook until mussels are just opened.

5. Discard any unopened mussels. Salt & pepper to taste.

HUNTER-GATHERER
900 MAIN STREET, COLUMBIA

"Beer is proof that God loves us and wants us to be happy."
Benjamin Franklin

121

A CELEBRATION OF
HUSK
SOUTHERN INGREDIENTS
RESTAURANT
CHARLESTON, SOUTH CAROLINA

CORNBREAD - WORD BURNING OVEN VERSION

Husk, transforms the essence of Southern food. Led by Chef Sean Brock and Chef de Cuisine Travis Grimes, the kitchen reinterprets the bounty of the surrounding area, exploring an ingredient-driven cuisine that begins in the rediscovery of heirloom products and redefines what it means to cook and eat in Charleston. Starting with a larder of ingredients indigenous to the South, and set within a building complex dating to the late 19th century, Brock crafts menus throughout the day, responding to what local purveyors are supplying the kitchen at any given moment. The restaurant is as casual as it is chic, evoking a way of life centered on seasonality and the grand traditions of Charleston life – one lived at a slower pace, preferably with a cocktail and a wide porch in the late afternoon.

**2 C. Anson Mills yellow cornmeal
1 ½ C. Cruz Family buttermilk
1 farm egg
½ tsp baking soda
½ tsp baking powder
4 Tbsp Benton's bacon fat
2 Tbsp Benton's bacon pieces**

1. Mix all the dry ingredients.

2. Mix all the wet ingredients except 1 Tbsp of bacon fat.

3. Place a cast iron skillet in the word burning oven until it's hot.

4. Add the 1 Tbsp of bacon fat to the skillet (it should sizzle).

5. Add the batter and cook for approximately 8 minutes. The oven should be about 800°F.

HUSK RESTAURANT
76 QUEEN STREET, CHARLESTON

"If it doesn't come from the South, it's not coming through the door. [It's] not about rediscovering Southern cooking, but exploring the reality of Southern food."
Chef Sean Brock

123

SHE-CRAB SOUP

Voted the Best Seafood Restaurant in the Southeast by Southern Living Magazine 9 years in a row. Hyman's is as much a part of Charleston as Charleston is a part of Hyman's. It's a fun family dining experience not to be missed when visiting Charleston

Signature Tastes of **SOUTH CAROLINA**

2 ½ C. milk
1 lb crabmeat
½ C. celery, finely diced
1 Tbsp chicken base
½ C. heavy cream
4 tsp sherry
½ onion, diced
2 ½ C. flour
1 stick butter

1. Sauté onions and celery with butter in a saucepan.

2. Add flour and stir until thick.

3. Add heavy cream and chicken base. Bring to a boil stirring occasionally.

4. Add crabmeat and simmer for 5 minutes.

5. Add milk to get desired consistency.

6. Top each serving with tsp of sherry.

Serves 4.

HYMAN'S SEAFOOD
215 MEETING STREET, CHARLESTON

"Sometimes I pray to Cod for the veal-power to stop playing with my food words, but I fear it's too bread into me. For all I know, the wurst may be yet to come."
Mark Morton, 'Arts & Scantlings' (Gastronomica, Fall 2006)

Maple & Bourbon Braised Caw Caw Creek Pork Loin Roast

Signature Tastes of SOUTH CAROLINA

Pork Loin Roast:
2 Caw Caw Creek pork loins
2 Tbsp unsalted butter
2 tsp fresh garlic, minced
3 Tbsp bourbon
¼ C. pure maple syrup
¾ C. demi-glace or brown gravy
Salt & pepper to taste

Onion Rings:
2 large sweet onions, such as Palmetto Sweets
2 C. buttermilk, well shaken
4 tsp salt
2 tsp black pepper
2 C. flour
4 C. peanut oil

Grits:
2 C. whole milk
½ C. white stone ground Adluh grits
1/3 lb unsalted butter
1 Tbsp chicken base
Salt & pepper to taste

Asparagus:
20 stalks of Asparagus, blanched
2 Tbsp butter
Salt & pepper to taste

Pork Loin Roast:
1. Heat butter in a deep skillet or braising pan over medium heat. Season pork with salt & pepper. Carefully place pork in hot pan. Cook about 8 minutes on each side. Remove pork from pan and place on cutting board; let cool for a few minutes. While pork is cooling, add garlic and maple to pan and let simmer for about 2 minutes. Add demi-glace and bourbon and let simmer 2 more minutes. Slice pork thinly off the bone and add back to pan. Cook over medium-low heat for about 10 minutes. Add bones and place in preheated 350°F oven and cook approximately 45 minutes. Remove from oven and season with salt & pepper.

Onion Rings:
1. Cut onions crosswise into ½" thick rings. Separate rings saving small inside rings for another use. Stir together buttermilk, 2 tsp salt and 1 tsp pepper in a large bowl. Gently stir in onion rings; let stand for about 10 minutes then drain in colander. Heat oil in fryer to 375°F. Whisk together flour and remaining salt & pepper in another bowl. Dredge onions a few at a time in flour mix and let stand in a single layer on a wax lined cookie sheet for 15 minutes. Fry onion rings in small batches till golden brown. Transfer when cooked to paper towel lined plate.

Grits:
1. Heat milk and butter over medium flame in a sauce pot. Once butter is melted, add grits stirring well for the first 4 minutes. Turn down flame and continue cooking for approximately 40 minutes, stirring often. Add chicken base about half-way through cooking. Salt & pepper to taste.

Asparagus:
1. Add butter to medium skillet over medium-high heat. Once melted, add asparagus and sauté for 2 minutes moving frequently in pan. Add salt & pepper to taste and toss asparagus in pan a few times.

To serve: Spoon about 5 oz. of grits into entree sized pasta bowl. Spoon 6 oz. of pork over top, then lay 5 stalks of asparagus on side of grits. Top it all off with crispy onion rings and serve. Serves 4.

640 E. Main Street, Ridge Springs JUNIPER

"I do not like onions. It's so funny because I am probably one of the least picky eaters ever. Pretty much any type of new food, I'll try it, I'll eat it. But onions, and pork. Pork and onions."
Stacie Orrico, Musician

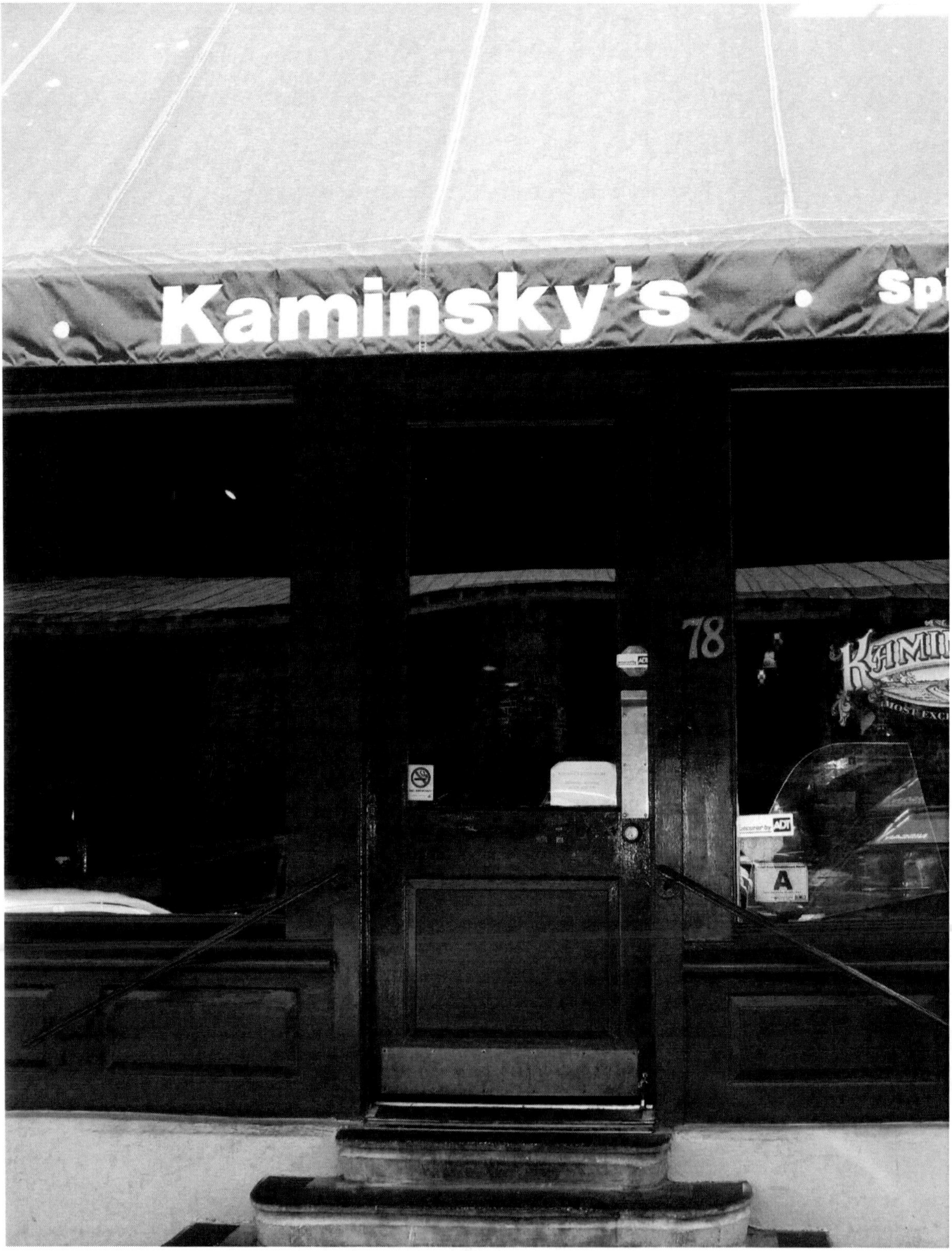

Kaminsky's
78

Signature Tastes of SOUTH CAROLINA

Our "most excellent" desserts are prepared fresh each day by our talented pastry chefs with selections changing daily. We encourage you to explore our selection of signature desserts housed in the case at the front door. Relax and enjoy your most excellent selection of dessert with a beverage. In addition to our vast array of specialty coffees, we also offer a full beer, wine and liquor selection.

Unsalted butter, for greasing
2 ¾ C. all-purpose flour, plus more for dusting
1 C. pecan pieces
3 ripe bananas, chopped
½ C. finely chopped fresh pineapple
1 tsp. ground cinnamon
1/2 tsp. freshly grated nutmeg
1/2 tsp. ground ginger
1 1/4 teaspoons baking soda
1/2 teaspoon salt
3 large eggs, at room temperature
1 3/4 cups granulated sugar
1 cup vegetable oil
For the Frosting:
2 packages cream cheese (8 ounces each), at room temperature
12 tablespoons unsalted butter, cubed, at room temperature
2 cups confectioners' sugar
1 tablespoon finely grated lemon zest
1 teaspoon vanilla

Make the cake:

1. Preheat the oven to 350 degrees F. Butter two 8-inch round cake pans and line with parchment paper. Butter the parchment and dust with flour.

2. Spread the pecans on a baking sheet and bake until fragrant and toasted, about 8 minutes. Let cool slightly, then roughly chop. Toss with the bananas, pineapple and ½ cup flour in a small bowl.

3. Whisk the remaining 2 ¼ cups flour, the cinnamon, nutmeg, ginger, baking soda and salt in a bowl. Beat the eggs and granulated sugar in a separate bowl with a mixer on high speed until thick and light, 5 minutes. Gradually beat in the vegetable oil.

4. Sprinkle the flour mixture over the egg mixture, then gently fold to make a thick batter. Fold in the pecan-fruit mixture, then transfer the batter to the prepared pans. Bake until the cakes are firm and a toothpick inserted into the middle comes out clean, 50 to 55 minutes. Cool in the pans on a rack, 25 minutes, then invert the cakes onto the rack to cool completely.

Make the frosting:

1. Beat the cream cheese in a large bowl with a mixer until fluffy, then gradually beat in the butter until combined. Sift the confectioners' sugar over the cream cheese mixture and beat until smooth. Add the lemon zest and vanilla and beat until light and fluffy.

2. Place one cake layer on a serving plate. Spread about half of the frosting on top, then cover with the other cake layer. Spread the remaining frosting over the top and sides of the cake.

KAMINSKY'S 78 N. MARKET STREET, CHARLESTON

A compromise is the art of dividing a cake in such a way that everyone believes he has the biggest piece.
Ludwig, Erhard, Politician

BIG CATCH
Lakeside Grill

TRIVIA THURS 7 PM
LIVE MUSIC
SAT AUG 14 8PM

CAROLINA BBQ QUAIL & SHRIMP

This restaurant is at the Lake Barnwell with plenty of parking. The food is great and try the seafood. Their prices are very reasonable and the service is good too. You order as you go in and you can choose to eat inside or outside..

Signature Tastes of SOUTH CAROLINA

4 quail, split
24 shrimp, peeled & deveined
2 Tbsp olive oil
1 Tbsp butter
2 Tbsp hot sauce
2 tsp smoked sweet paprika
1 Tbsp brown sugar
1 Tbsp black pepper
2 Tbsp garlic salt
½ C. green onions, diced
¼ C. bell peppers, diced
½ C. BBQ sauce
4 servings, hot cooked grits
1 C. white cheddar cheese, shredded
¼ C. half & half

1. Mix together the sweet paprika, brown sugar, black pepper and garlic salt to make a seasoning rub for quail. Season the quail liberally on both sides with rub.

2. Place quail on a preheated outdoor grill or on a preheated cast iron indoor grill pan. Grill for approximately 20 minute or until done, turning every 4-5 minutes.

3. While the quail are cooking, melt butter with olive oil in a sauté pan. Place shrimp in pan, along with the green onions and bell peppers, cooking until the shrimp turn pink. Do not overcook.

4. Add hot sauce and BBQ sauce. Let cook until the sauce caramelizes in the pan on the shrimp. Remove pan from heat and set aside. During the last 7 minutes or so of cooking, brush the quail with remaining BBQ sauce.

5. Serve over white cheddar cheese grits. For each serving, place ¼ of grits on the plate, then top with 8 BBQ shrimp, 1 quail and some sauce from the pan.

LAKESIDE GRILLE
188 GILMORE STREET, BARNWELL

"Nothing would be more tiresome than eating and drinking if God had not made them a pleasure as well as a necessity."
Voltaire

TENDERLOIN BITES WITH CHIPOTLE AIOLI

Larkin's strives to exceed our guests' expectations and be the best destination dining facility in the Carolinas. Larkin's on the River was established in October of 2005 and since that time, Larkin's culinary inspirations have been created by none other than, Executive Chef Alex Castro – known to our associates and guests as "Chef Alex." He has taken what was once an old school steakhouse and evolved it into one of the most stunning and sensational restaurants in all of South Carolina. Chef Alex has a keen sense for flavors, colors and composition. His creations have entertained diners in Greenville for the past 19 years and his ability to present a flavorful, beautiful and captivating plate every time is what makes Chef Alex an accomplished culinary professional.

Tenderloin Bites:
1 ½ lbs tenderloin
¼ C. fresh cilantro, chopped
½ tsp cumin
¼ tsp curry powder
2 Tbsp garlic, chopped
2 Tbsp Worcestershire sauce
¼ C. fresh lime juice
¼ C. red wine vinegar
¾ C. olive oil
¼ tsp cracked black pepper
Dash of salt

Chipotle Aioli:
1 whole egg
1 egg yolk
1 garlic clove, diced fine
2 oz. chipotle pepper (with sauce from the can)
1 lemon, juiced
1 ½ C. vegetable oil
¼ tsp salt
Dash of salt

Tenderloin Bites:
1. Chop the beef into ½" cubes.
2. In a bowl, mix the cilantro, cumin, curry powder, garlic and Worcestershire sauce with the lime juice and vinegar.
3. Toss the beef in the vinegar mixture and then toss in the oil.
4. Season with salt & black pepper.
5. Let marinate in the refrigerator for at least 1 hour (can be left overnight).

Chipotle Aioli:
1. Place egg, egg yolk, garlic, chipotle pepper and lemon juice in a stainless steel bowl.
2. Whisk vigorously, adding the oil in a slow steady stream (to make an "emulsion" – should look like mayonnaise when finished). Season with salt.

Preparation:
1. Sear the steak bites in a hot skillet over medium-high heat, to desired temperature. We like to serve them medium rare.
2. Serve with the Chipotle Aioli for dipping. A good accompaniment is pita chips or garlic crostini.

LARKIN'S ON THE RIVER
318 S. MAIN STREET, GREENVILLE

"Beef is the soul of cooking."
Marie-Antoine Carême

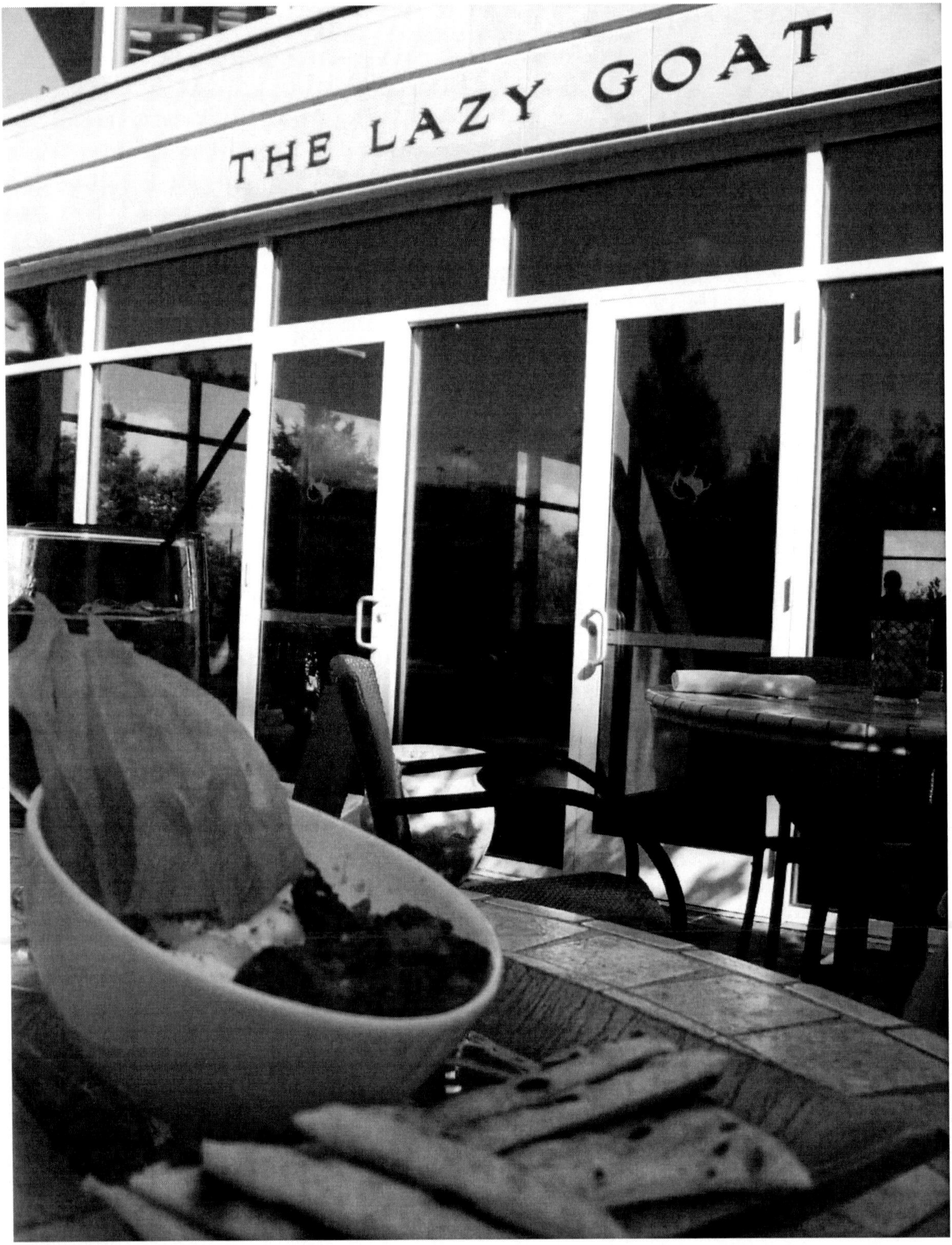
THE LAZY GOAT

The Lazy Goat is a Mediterranean-themed restaurant with a menu featuring global influences from Spain, Morocco, Italy, France, Greece, Africa and the Middle East. Chef Vicky Moore and her team are known for a "made from scratch" approach to cooking – from the "zahtar" on the table to the house made pasta, every item served is almost exclusively made by the culinary team. A dining experience designed around taking your time, and sharing great food and stories. Guests are invited to leave behind responsibility and worry while they try a little bit of this and a little bit of that – or a whole lot of whatever they like. Whatever your pleasure, The Lazy Goat is truly time well wasted.

Sofrito Broth:
1 medium red onion, diced
6 cloves garlic, smashed
1 medium red bell pepper, seeds removed & diced
1 medium yellow bell pepper, seeds removed & diced
1 serrano chile, roughly chopped with seeds
6 medium Roma tomatoes, roughly chopped with seeds
¼ C. white wine
¼ C. sherry
¼ C. cream
½ bunch cilantro, torn in half
Pinch saffron
2 qt. vegetable or chicken stock
Salt & pepper to taste

Paella:
3 Tbsp olive oil
2 C. Arborio rice
8 oz. pamplona Spanish chorizo, sliced thin
¼ C. shallots, finely minced
½ C. roasted peppers, diced
1 C. cherry tomatoes, halved
8 asparagus spears, trimmed & blanched
12 snow peas, trimmed & blanched
8 large prawns, deveined
12 calamari tubes & tentacles

Sofrito Broth:
1. Heat a large sauté pan until smoking hot. Very carefully add olive oil. Add the red onion and crushed garlic, stirring constantly for 2 minutes until slightly charred.
2. Add the bell peppers and serrano chile and continue to cook on high heat for 3 minutes.
3. Add the tomatoes and allow to cook for 7 minutes or until all of the liquid has evaporated. Season generously with salt & pepper.
4. Once the tomatoes have cooked down, add the white wine and sherry and reduce by half.
5. Add the heavy cream and saffron, bringing to a boil. Once boiling, turn off the heat and add the torn cilantro. Allow the mixture to cool. Once cool, transfer to a blender and blend.
6. In a large pot, heat the stock to boiling and reduce to a simmer. Slowly add the sofrito to the stock whisking constantly. Allow to simmer while you prepare the rest of the paella.

Paella:
1. Heat a large sauté pan over medium heat. Add olive oil to the pan and sauté the shallots.
2. Once the shallots are translucent, add the Arborio rice and chorizo to the pan stirring constantly as in the preparation of risotto.
3. Gradually add the stock, ladle by ladle, stirring constantly until all of the liquid is absorbed and the rice is tender.
4. Turn off the heat and add the roasted peppers, cherry tomatoes, asparagus and snow peas. Season with salt & pepper.
5. Season the calamari and prawns with salt & pepper and grill or sauté in a separate pan.
6. Transfer the paella to a large serving dish and top with the grilled seafood. Serve with toasted baguettes.

THE LAZY GOAT
170 RIVER PLACE, GREENVILLE

"The Creator, by making man eat to live, invites him to do so with appetite and rewards him with pleasure."
Jean-Anthelme Brillat-Savarin,
'The Physiology of Taste'

BEER BREAD

Built soon after the Municipal Marina opened, The Marina Variety Store Restaurant and the Altine family have been serving Charleston's favorite local dishes since 1963. The Variety Store offers breakfast, lunch and dinner to locals and visitors alike with views of the Charleston City Marina that are unmatched. Try one of The Variety Store's famous benedicts for breakfast, a juicy 8 oz. burger for lunch, or a heaping seafood platter for dinner. Don't forget Mike Altine, Jr.'s legendary crab dip to kick things off. The Variety Store also offers first class catering for weddings and corporate events throughout the Lowcountry.

4 ½ cans beer (your choice)
3 C. sugar
4 oz. honey
1 oz. vanilla
3 oz. butter, melted
8 C. self-rising flour
Honey butter

1. Mix first 4 ingredients and let rest for 15 minutes.

2. Slowly incorporate flour and butter until well blended.

3. Pour into 3 greased bread loaf pans.

4. Cook in convection oven at 350°F for 50 minutes. Conventional oven times may vary.

5. Serve warm with honey butter.

MARINA VARIETY STORE RESTAURANT
17 LOCKWOOD DRIVE, CHARLESTON

"Why beer is better than wine... human feet are conspicuously absent from beer making."
Steve Mirsky, Scientific American (May, 2007)

CAROLINA GOLD BBQ SAUCE

Maurice Bessinger, founder of Piggy Park, inherited his Gourmet Blend BBQ Sauce recipe and his restaurant expertise from his father, Joseph Bessinger. Joseph began the small family BBQ business in 1939 in Holly Hill, SC. Maurice's father was known as Big Joe, and Maurice and his brothers were known as Little Joes. With 70 years in the BBQ business, Maurice retired at age 80, and now his sons, daughters and grandchildren run the various business enterprises. The restaurant recipe itself is a closely guarded secret, but we have it on good authority that this is as close as a home chef can get.

2 Tbsp granulated onion powder
½ C. yellow mustard
½ C. brown sugar
½ C. cider vinegar
1 Tbsp dry mustard
1 teaspoon cayenne
1 bay leaf
Salt to taste

1. Combine all the ingredients, except the bay leaf, in a large sauce pan.

2. Using an immersion blender, blend the ingredient until smooth and completely incorporated.

3. Slowly simmer for 30 minutes, using the blender to uniformly heat the sauce.

4. Add the bay leaf for the last 5 minutes of simmering. Do not use the blender but stir with a spoon.

5. Remove the bay leaf and allow to cool and use. Can be stored in the refrigerator for up to six months.

MAURICE'S BBQ

MULTIPLE LOCATIONS ACROSS THE STATE

People ask me, "Where's the best barbecue?"
I tell them, "the best barbecue is any place that I am"
John Willingham, Willinghams Chapionship BBQ

FRAPPES
frozen
espresso beverage
topped w/ whipped cream

- DARK CHOCOLATE
- MILK CHOCOLATE
- WHITE CHOCOLATE
- VANILLA
- SUGAR-FREE VANILLA

16oz 3.65   24oz 4.35

FRAPTACULARS
amazing coffee-less
frappes.

16oz 3.65   24oz 3.75

FRUIT SMOOTHIES
100% fruit

- STRAWBERRY
- STRAWBERRY-BANANA
- FOUR-BERRY
- MANGO
- MANGO-STRAWBERRY

16oz 3.95   20oz 4.55

ADD-INS (55¢)
- peanut butter   - yogurt
- extra espresso - flax seed
- supplements: MULTI-VITAMIN
                ENERGY-BOOST
- oreos   vanilla
- spinach   WHEY PROTEIN
- natural morin syrups (65¢)

FLAVORED SYRUPS
VANILLA   FROSTED MINT
CARAMEL   DARK BERRY
HAZELNUT   RASPBERRY
IRISH CREME   BLUEBERRY
MACCHIATO   POMEGRANATE-
ALMOND   STRAWBERRY
               COCONUT

ORGANIC TEAS
- ASP GREEN   HERBAL
- EARL GREY   CINN ORANGE
- BREAKFAST   PEPPERMINT
- MOROCCAN   LEM GINGER
- SPICED CHAI   INDIAN SPICE
- ROOIBOS   AARANG
                 PUMPKIN BERRY

CUSTOM GIFT
BASKETS

CREAMY CUCUMBER DILL SOUP

Come into the Midnight Rooster and let us brighten your mornings even earlier with our full-service breakfast. Sit down and enjoy one of our freshly made crepes, omelets, on-the-go breakfast sandwiches, or already famous Belgian waffles along with your ritual latte or cup of Joe. Serving breakfast, lunch and dinner, we're sure to have something for everyone. Great for your early morning business meetings or family gatherings.

3 large cucumbers, peeled, seeded & chopped
1 Vidalia onion, chopped
2 Tbsp fresh dill, chopped
3 C. vegetable stock
½ C. heavy cream

1. Place cucumber, onion, dill and vegetable stock in a saucepan. Bring to a boil on medium-high heat.

2. Reduce heat to simmer and cook until cucumber and onion are tender.

3. Allow to cool and puree using a food processor or blender.

4. Place back in saucepan, add heavy cream and reheat slowly (do not boil).

5. Serve chilled with side of The Midnight Rooster's crostini or other delicious crisp bread.

MIDNIGHT ROOSTER
136 E. CAROLINA AVENUE, HARTSVILLE

The cucumber is ".... about as close to neutrality as a vegetable can get without ceasing to exist."
Waverley Root

Fried Oysters with Mango Salsa & Red Pepper Aioli

Located just a few miles from Camden and a short 30 minute ride from Columbia, we offer a unique and serene dining experience unlike anything else in the state! Though our steaks are our claim to fame, we offer a full variety of American cuisine amidst historic and incredibly scenic surroundings.

Oysters:
1 dz. oysters, shucked
½ C. Boykin Mill cornmeal
¼ C. Panko bread crumbs
1/3 C. all-purpose flour
Salt & pepper to taste
3 C. vegetable oil

Mango Salsa:
1 large ripe mango, diced
1 small red onion, finely diced
1 small red pepper, finely diced
1 small green pepper, finely diced
1 each lemon & lime, juiced
1 Tbsp parsley, chopped
1/3 C. red wine vinegar
1 Tbsp fresh cilantro, chopped
Salt & Pepper to taste
3 Tbsp sugar
1 clove garlic, minced

Aioli:
1 large red bell pepper
1 lemon, juiced
1 C. mayo
Salt & pepper to taste
1 Tbsp fresh parsley

Oysters:
1. Heat oil in cast iron skillet to about 400°F. Whisk all dry ingredients in a bowl with salt & pepper until combined. Dredge oysters until well coated and drop in cornmeal mixture. Fry for approximately 2-3 minutes and place on dry paper towel to drain.

Mango Salsa:
1. Add peppers, onions, sugar and vinegar in a small sauce pot. Heat on medium to high heat until slightly reduced. Cool for 10-20 minutes. In a small bowl, add mango, parsley, the lemon and lime, pepper and onion mixture, cilantro, garlic and salt & pepper. Mix until all ingredients are well combined.

Aioli:
1. Roast pepper in the oven at 475°F for about 10-15 minutes until soft. Pull out stem, seed and peel off skin. Puree until smooth in blender. Add puree to a small bowl with remaining ingredients and whisk together until blended.

To serve: Pour aioli in a squeeze bottle and decorate plate with aioli. Place a good portion of salsa in the middle of plate and arrange oysters in a circle around the salsa. Garnish with chopped chives and paprika.

The Mill Pond Steakhouse
84 Boykin Mill Road, Rembert

"I prefer my oysters fried; that way I know my oysters died."
Roy Blount, Jr.

CORN PUDDING

Signature Tastes of

Since opening in 1989, Motor Supply – in the heart of the Congaree Vista – has become a favorite among locals and visitors alike. We serve up some of the freshest and most innovative food in town with menus changing not once, but twice daily! All within the unique setting of a renovated engine supply building from the late 1800's, now listed on the National Register of Historic Places. Just look for the original 1930s neon sign! In keeping with the long history of the location, we strive to use local ingredients with classic from scratch techniques. Motor Supply (known as 'Motor' to locals) offers an extensive selection of wines carefully tasted and hand-picked for your enjoyment. As one of Columbia's first bistros and first restaurant in the Vista, Motor Supply is proud to celebrate its 19th anniversary this year. Our sincerest wish is to continue to provide a first-class dining experience in a comfortable atmosphere you'll enjoy with family and friends again and again.

5 ears corn, stripped of husk & silk
1/3 C. sugar
1 ½ tsp sea salt
1 Tbsp all-purpose flour
3 eggs, beaten
1 C. milk
1 C. heavy cream
¼ C. butter, melted
½ tsp nutmeg, freshly grated

1. Preheat oven to 350°F.
2. Cut corn from cob, slicing from the top of the ear to the base trying not to cut too deeply.
3. Using the blade of the knife, scrape the remaining corn from the cob, aka milking the cob.
4. Sprinkle corn in dry ingredients slowly while mixing. Mix well.
5. Beat eggs, milk and cream together and add to corn mixture while stirring.
6. Blend in melted butter and ladle into a 6 cup casserole dish.
7. Place casserole dish into a pan of water and place into preheated oven for about 40 minutes or until golden brown and set. To test, insert the blade of a knife into the center of the pudding; if the blade comes out clean, it's done.

Pairing suggestions: French Sauvignon Blanc a Sancerre would be perfect because of its minerality and mild acid to help with the richness, or Sweet Tea...just because.

MOTOR SUPPLY COMPANY BISTRO
920 GERVAIS STREET, COLUMBIA

"Salt is born of the purest of parents: the sun and the sea."
Pythagoras

FLASH FRIED YELLOW ADLUH GRITS

Founded in the early 80's as a sandwich and cookie shop, Mr. Friendly's New Southern Cafe has evolved into much more since its inception. Since 1995, we've been serving new Southern cuisine in a sophisticated, yet casual environment using only the freshest ingredients and simple preparations. There are always ocean-fresh fish and seafood specials, as well as innovative meat, poultry and wild game dishes. Our wine list is extensive and has won "Wine Spectator's Award of Excellence" ten times. We also have a wide variety of micro-brew beer, small batch Bourbon, flavored Vodkas and single-malt Scotch. Our concept is simple: great food, great service and great wine!

Signature Tastes of SOUTH CAROLINA

MR. FRIENDLY'S NEW SOUTHERN CAFÉ

2001-A GREEN STREET, COLUMBIA

3 ½ qt. water
2 oz. Mr. Friendly's Lowcountry seasoning (or your favorite Cajun seasoning)
2 oz. chicken base
1 bunch green onions, sliced
4 C. Adluh yellow grits
Roasted garlic
Goat cheese
Fresh herbs

1. Bring first 4 ingredients to a boil in 8 quart stock pot.

2. Whisk in grits and bring back to boil, stirring often.

3. Reduce heat and simmer until very thick, stirring often.

4. Pour into ½ sized sheet pan and allow to cool to room temperature.

5. Once solid after cooling, cut into 4 rows of 5 rectangles, then half each rectangle into wedges.

6. Remove each triangle carefully, dust with flour and deep fry for 4-5 minutes in 375°F oil.

7. Top with soft roasted garlic, goat cheese & fresh herbs.

"One cannot think well, love well, sleep well, if one has not dined well."
Virginia Woolf, English novelist, 'A Room of One's Own'

Cilantro Pesto Crusted Ahi Tuna

Signature Tastes of SOUTH CAROLINA

NANTUCKET SEAFOOD GRILL
40 W. BROAD STREET, GREENVILLE

Cilantro Pesto:
1 bunch cilantro
1 oz. fresh ginger, peeled
½ C. fresh basil
¼ C. macadamia nuts, toasted
5 sprigs mint
2 cloves garlic
Blended oil, as needed
Salt & pepper to taste

Coconut Jasmine Pilaf:
4 C. jasmine rice
13 oz. coconut milk
6 oz. pineapple juice
45 oz. water
1 oz. ginger, peeled & smashed
4 tsp salt
1 lime, zest

Pineapple Relish:
1 fresh pineapple, small dice
¼ C. shallot, small dice
6 sprigs mint, chopped
¼ bunch cilantro, chopped
½ oz. fresh ginger, grated

Cilantro Pesto Crusted Ahi Tuna:
6 8 oz. Ahi Tuna fillets
3 oz. cilantro pesto
6 C. coconut jasmine pilaf
3 oz. pineapple relish
6 oz. sweet chili vinaigrette
Salt & pepper to taste

Cilantro Pesto:
1. Combine everything except the oil in a food processor. Slowly add the oil until everything is incorporated.

Coconut Jasmine Pilaf:
1. Combine all ingredients in a 2" baking pan. Cover with foil and bake at 375°F for approximately 17 minutes. Fluff with a fork and discard ginger.

Pineapple Relish:
1. Combine all ingredients.

Cilantro Pesto Crusted Ahi Tuna:
1. Preheat the grill to medium-high heat. Season tuna with salt & pepper. Apply the pesto to one side of the tuna. Grill for 1 minute on each side for a rare fish.
2. Slice the tuna as thin as possible and serve over 1 cup of the jasmine rice. Top with 1 Tbsp of pineapple relish and 2 Tbsp of sweet chili vinaigrette.

Boss Lady's Chicken Salad

Since 1995 the New Moon Café has been serving up creative comfort food using fresh, local ingredients. Everything we serve is authentic food. We roast our own coffee in small batches, bake our breads and pastries in house, and make our soups from scratch every day. Outstanding food doesn't have to be complicated and expensive; it just requires a devotion to creating genuine food in an extraordinary way. We've been using locally sourced ingredients since way before it was fashionable. Not because we're trying to be trendsetters, it just makes good sense to cook with the freshest food available. It's good for the local economy, good for the environment, and really good on your plate!

1 ½ C. heavy mayo
2 Tbsp Greek seasoning
4 Tbsp lemon juice
6 C. chopped, cooked chicken
4 celery ribs, diced
1 ½ C. sweetened, dried cranberries
1 1/3 C. slivered almonds, toasted

1. Combine and whisk the mayo, seasoning and lemon juice.

2. Bake the almonds at 350°F for 5-7 minutes. Let cool.

3. Add the almonds and remaining ingredients to the mayo mixture, mixing well.

THE NEW MOON CAFÉ
118 LAURENS STREET, AIKEN

"Chicken salad has a certain glamour about it. Like the little black dress, it is chic and adaptable anywhere."
Laurie Colwin, 'Home Cooking'

Souvlaki-Pork Tenderloin Skewers

Both locations (Mount Gallant and India Hook) are wonderful. The food is consistently amazing and there is such a wide variety that you can please everyone in the family. Their Greek Salad with Souvlaki is wonderful.

1 Tbsp sea salt
1 pinch black pepper
¾ Tbsp fresh garlic
½ Tbsp fresh oregano
1 oz. lemon juice, freshly squeezed
2 oz. premium dry white wine
4 oz. olive oil
Pork tenderloin, sliced

1. Combine all the ingredients and blend well for 5 minutes.

2. Pour marinade over sliced pork tenderloin and marinate for 2 hours.

3. Place meat lengthwise on a water logged wooden skewer.

4. Grill skewers over an open flame char broiler.

706 Mt. Gallant Road & 727 Dilworth Lane, Rock Hill

Nishie G's

"Grilling means good times, good friends, and hopefully, great food."
Bobby Flay, celebrity chef, restaurateur

HOUSE MADE PAPPARDELLE PASTA

Signature Tastes of SOUTH CAROLINA

OAK STEAKHOUSE
17 BROAD STREET, CHARLESTON

Homemade Pappardelle Pasta:
8 egg yolks
3 C. all-purpose flour
1 C. Semolina flour
½ C. water
2 Tbsp extra virgin olive oil

Basil Pesto:
2 bunches basil
1 C. arugula
1 C. spinach
½ C. pine nuts, toasted
½ C. parmesan cheese, fresh grated
1 C. extra virgin olive oil
Salt & pepper to taste

Grilled Smoked Bacon:
½ lb double smoked bacon

House Made Parpadelle Pasta:
1 C. English peas
4 Tbsp basil pesto
Homemade pasta
1 C. pork belly
2 Tbsp parmesan cheese, fresh grated
Salt & pepper to taste

Homemade Pappardelle Pasta:
1. Combine egg yolks, all-purpose flour and Semolina flour together. Once mixed, slowly knead in water and olive oil. Continue to knead for 5 minutes. Cover the dough with lightly dampened towel and let rest for 1 hour in the refrigerator.
2. Once dough is rested, gradually roll down to the #4 setting in a standard pasta roller. Proceed to slice pasta down to 8-10" strips, approximately ¾" wide. Cook pasta for approximately 4 minutes, or until al dente. Once cooked, drain the pasta and set aside.

Basil Pesto:
1. Blanche all greens (basil, arugula & spinach) by cooking them in boiling water for approximately 15 seconds and immediately placing them in an ice bath (bowl of ice water). Squeeze all water out of the greens and rough chop them in a food processor.
2. Add toasted pine nuts and grated parmesan gradually while chopping the mixture together. Proceed to slowly add the extra virgin olive oil for consistency. Salt & pepper to taste.

Grilled Smoked Bacon:
1. Cut bacon into ¼" strips. Grill or sauté until most of the fat is rendered out (approximately 3" on each side). Chop into small cubes and set aside.

House Made Parpadelle Pasta:
1. Boil English peas for 1 minute. Drain and set aside. Fold basil pesto into the homemade pasta, followed by English peas and pork belly. Garnish with fresh grated parmesan cheese and season with salt & pepper. Serves 4

"Life is too short, and I'm Italian. I'd much rather eat pasta and drink wine than be a size 0."
Sophia Bush, Actress

155

CHILLED LOCAL PEACH & ROSEBANK FARMS CORN SOUP

The Ocean Room offers an unparalleled dining experience sure to please the most discriminating epicurean. Nathan Thurston, Chef of The Ocean Room, has been a member of the culinary team since opening in 2004. Chef Thurston and team specialize in the preparation of local, grass-fed beef from Mibek Farms in Barnwell and support local agriculture by writing seasonal menus based on availability of fresh produce. Chef Thurston is very active in the competitive culinary realm, and in addition to his role at The Sanctuary, he serves as Chairman of the Board for The Greater Charleston American Culinary Federation and teaches Southern Cuisine and European Cuisine at The Art Institute of Charleston.

**2 ears Rosebank Farms corn
3 C. vegetable stock
2 shallots, minced
¼ bunch thyme, tied
1 ¼ tsp sea salt
2 ½ C. peaches, skin on, diced
2 dashes peach bitters
½ tsp peach aroma
8 oz. simple syrup**

1. Shave corn off cobs. Scrape the cobs with the back of your knife, and place the corn, pulp and cobs in a sauce pot.

2. Add stock, shallots, thyme and sea salt, bring to a simmer.

3. Continue simmering until the corn is tender. Remove thyme and corn cobs from the broth and discard.

4. Add diced peaches and return to a simmer for 5 minutes.

5. Remove from heat and place in a blender. Process until well combined and add simple syrup with the motor still running.

6. Adjust seasoning with additional fine sea salt. Adjust consistency with additional simple syrup if too thick. Chill overnight.

Recommended Garnishes:
Seared Foie Gras
Fresh Peach Slice
Charred & Shaved Corn
Homemade Granola
Edible Flowers

"My philosophy is to strive for excellence in every aspect that I endeavor. Embracing this philosophy commits me to utilizing the finest local and artisan ingredients available to craft my southern cuisine."
Chef Nathan Thurston

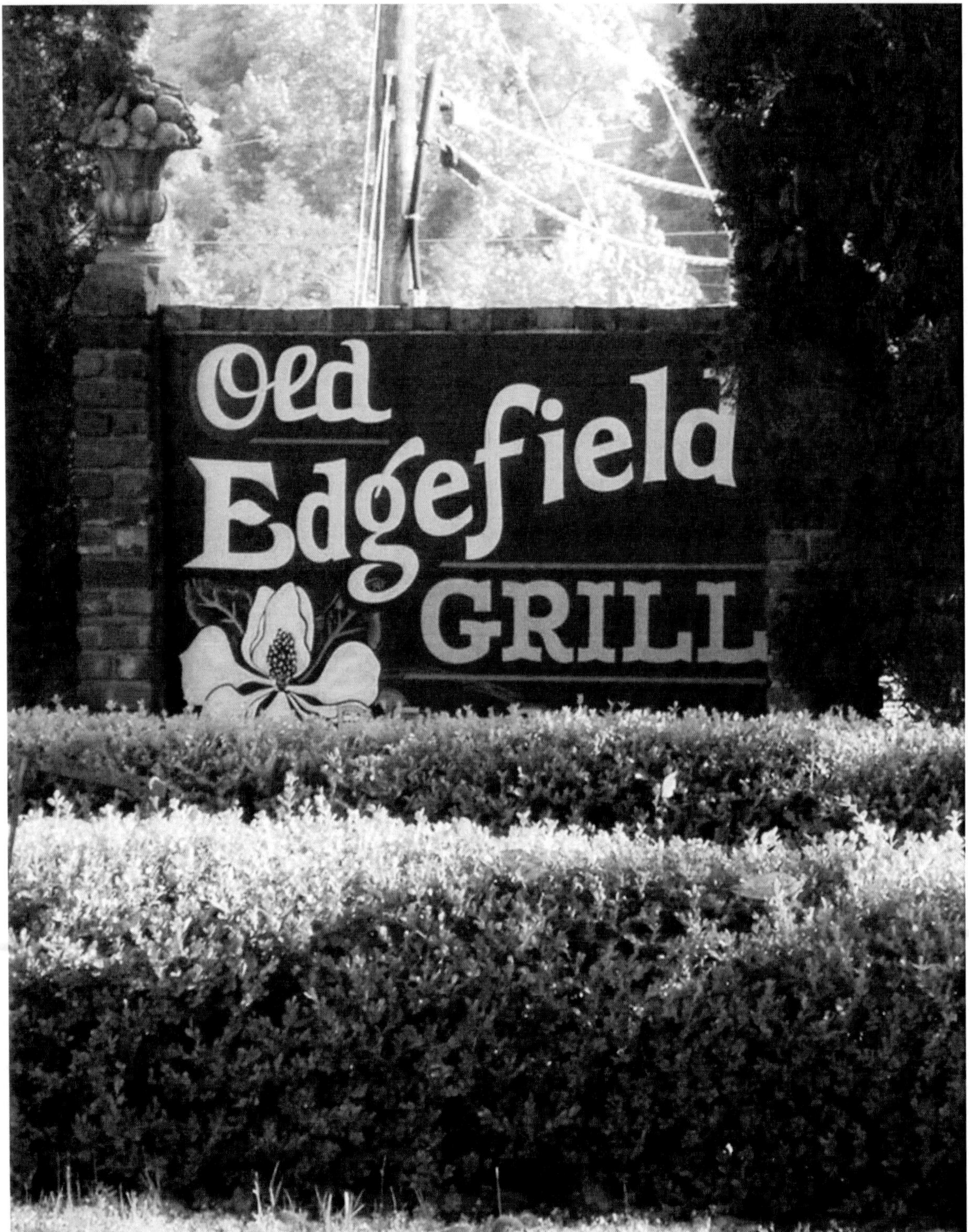
Old
Edgefield
GRILL

CREAMY SWEET VIDALIA ONION SOUP & PEACH MERINGUE

The Old Edgefield Grill, located right off the historic town square in Edgefield, is one of the best fine dining establishments in the region. We've provided fine Southern foods in an historic and architecturally-significant house for more than a decade. We're always focused on serving the highest quality food in a delightful and elegant, yet comfortably casual atmosphere. Whether you're looking for the most tender and tasty steaks, the finest fresh seafood or any number of other delectable entrees, the Grill will surpass your expectations and be among the most memorable dining experiences of your life.

Onion Soup:
2 cloves garlic, minced
2 qt. Vidalia onions, chopped
1 C. white wine
¼ stick butter
½ C. all-purpose flour
1 qt. chicken stock
1 qt. water
2 Tbsp white vinegar
½ pt. heavy cream
Salt & white pepper to taste
Apple juice
Croutons (optional)

Peach Meringue:
Fresh peeled, sliced peaches
Baked meringue rosettes
Vanilla ice cream
Raspberry sorbet
Whipped cream
Fresh mint
Powder sugar

Onion Soup:
1. Simmer onions, garlic, wine and butter, covered over low heat for 10 minutes. Stir in flour to incorporate.

2. Add chicken stock, water and vinegar. Cook uncovered for approximately 20 minutes to thicken, stirring occasionally.

3. Add heavy cream and adjust seasoning with salt & white pepper.

4. Puree soup and add some apple juice. Strain and serve with mint sprigs. This soup is better when allowed to rest overnight. Soup can be served chilled.

Peach Meringue:
1. Assemble in layers. Place a little whipped cream on serving dish, then place meringue on cream to prevent sliding.

2. Place ½ scoop of each ice cream and sorbet on meringue. Top with whipped cream. Add peaches to top and surrounding area.

3. Sprinkle with sugar. Place mint sprig on side of dessert.

THE OLD EDGEFIELD GRILL
202 PENN STREET, EDGEFIELD

"An onion can make people cry but there's never been a vegetable that can make people laugh."
Will Rogers, Entertainer

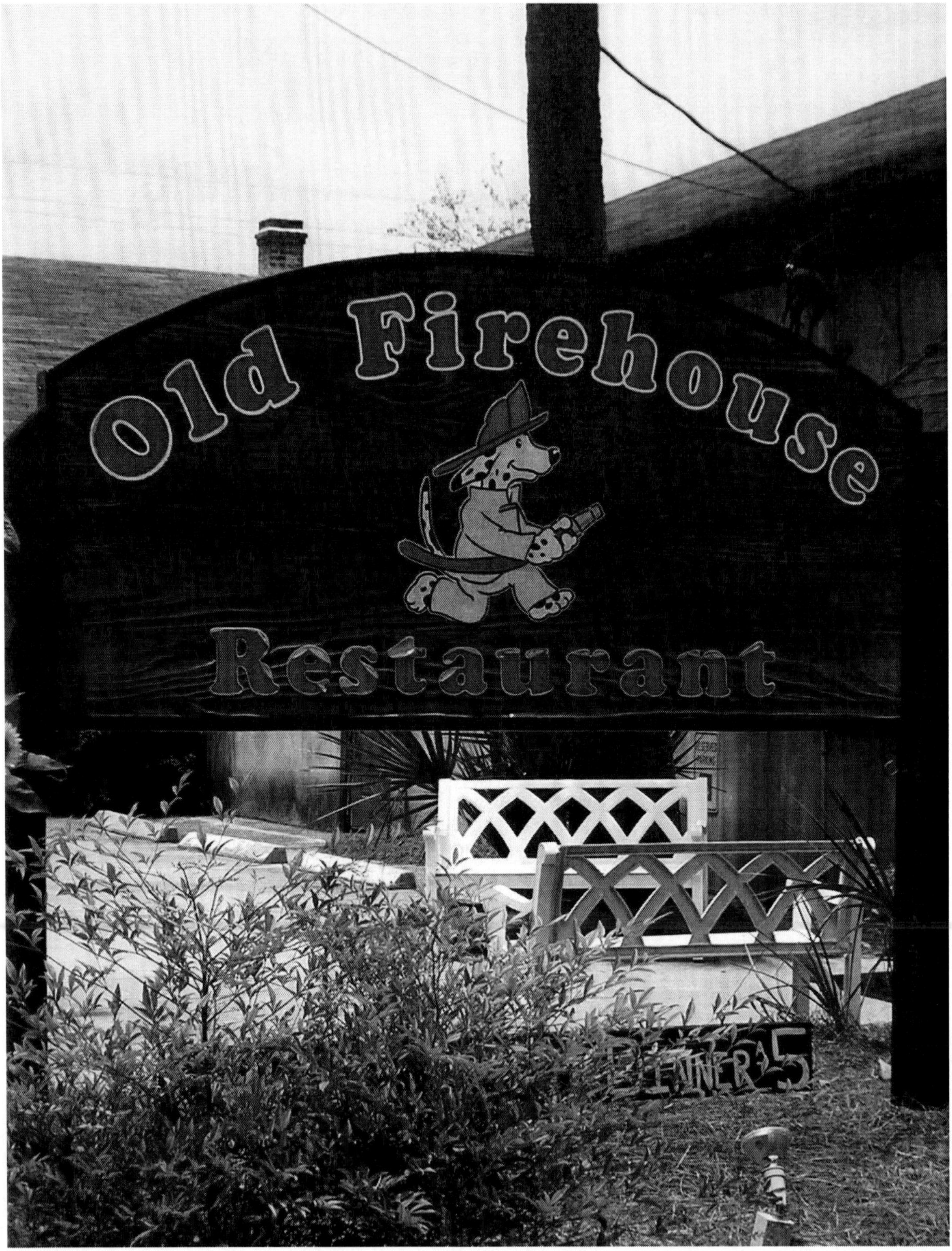
Old Firehouse
Restaurant

SHRIMP SUCCOTASH

Welcome to the Old FireHouse Restaurant, located in the heart of Hollywood! We sit inside the original St. Pauls fire station and have transformed where the trucks used to park into an open kitchen, bar and seating area. As you enter the dining room, look up because the doors still hang from the ceiling! We're a casual restaurant that specializes in local seafood and produce. We're always changing our menu and trying new things so that your dining experience will never grow old. Our regular customers enjoy the variety of the menu where they can choose from local seafood, pork chops from Orangeburg, top quality steaks and some good old-fashioned southern soul food. We're a small town restaurant that loves good food and wine. In the winter we may close a little early if it's slow and in the summer we may stay open a little late. Come to the Old FireHouse and enjoy good food, good spirits, and good times.

2 Tbsp olive oil
1 C. medium Vidalia sweet onion, small dice
1 C. medium red bell pepper, rib removed, small dice
1 C. sweet corn, 4 ears
1-2 lbs shrimp 26/30, peeled & deveined
1 lb cooked butterbeans, speckled butterbeans, or crowder peas (save potlikker)
2-3 C. cooked jasmine rice (2 C. dry rice & 3 C. water/stock)
1 bunch green onions, finely sliced
Hot sauce

1. Cook butterbeans and jasmine rice. We like to cook the butterbeans with a whole onion julienned, bacon or ham hock, and water. To cook the rice, bring the water to a boil, add the rice, stir, cover and bring the liquid back to a boil. Turn off and leave on the burner. If you want really great rice, substitute potlikker for water when cooking rice. Once done, set to the side.

2. In a large sauté pan, add olive oil and heat. Add sweet onion, bell pepper and sweet corn. Sauté for about 5 minutes until onion is a little translucent.

3. Add shrimp and sauté for about 4 minutes.

4. Add as many butterbeans as you like (start with a cup) as well as some of the potlikker. This dish should be moist, not wet and the potlikker will help finish cooking the shrimp.

5. Add rice and cover. Reduce heat and simmer until shrimp are cooked.

6. Serve in bowls and garnish with hot sauce and green onions.

Serves 4-6

"I met a keen observer who gave me a tip: 'If you run across a restaurant where you often see priests eating with priests, or sporting girls with sporting girls, you may be confident that it is good. Those are two classes of people who like to eat well and get their money's worth.'"
A.J. Liebling (columnist)

SALMON EN CROUTE

Built on the site of an original oyster cannery, the Old Oyster Factory is a delight for family and children of all ages. Enjoy superb, innovative seafood and steaks while taking in one of the Lowcountry's best panoramic views of the marshland landscape. From 1925 until the 1990's, 1,700 acres of nearby creeks and wetlands were harvested by local oystermen and their yield brought to a one-story concrete building located directly under the restaurant. After canning, the oysters were shipped all over the Lowcountry. Small family-owned boats can still be seen today navigating the eddies off of Broad Creek, continuing the tradition of generations. Indeed, names like Mitchell and Pinckney, descendants of the original working oyster families, grace nearby mailboxes. At the Old Oyster Factory, we're surrounded by tradition on all sides, and we look forward to sharing our heritage with you.

1 lb salmon, diced
½ lb scallops, diced
½ lb medium shrimp, peeled & deveined
4 oz. crab meat
3 tsp mayo
4 (5"x5") sheets of puff pastry
4 fresh spinach leaves
Fresh chopped dill to taste
Dash of lemon juice
Worcestershire sauce to taste
White & black pepper to taste
Fresh chopped garlic to taste
Egg yolks

1. Mix scallops and shrimp.

2. Add crabmeat, mayo, dill and seasonings.

3. Place spinach leaf on a puff pastry square and add a slice of salmon.

4. Place about 4 oz. of seafood mixture on top and add another slice of salmon.

5. Pull ends of puff pastry together and place on a baking sheet.

6. Brush with egg yolk and bake at 350°F for 20 minutes. Enjoy!

Serves 4

OLD OYSTER FACTORY
101 MARSHLAND ROAD, HILTON HEAD ISLAND

"I think we're going to the moon because it's in the nature of the human being to face challenges. It's by the nature of his deep inner soul... we're required to do these things just as salmon swim upstream."
Neil Armstrong, Astronaut

ORANGE & SOY ROASTED PORK MEDALLIONS

The Old Post Office Restaurant is a popular meeting place for Edistonians and guests alike. It's the site of both the former U.S Post Office and Bailey's General Store. We feature an excellent menu of Lowcountry specialties and regional favorites. Popular menu items include the Orange & Soy Roasted Pork Medallions served over fragrant jasmine rice, OPO Crab Cakes full of lump crab, baked until risen and lightly drizzled with Mousseline Sauce, and the famous stone ground grits which are slow-cooked all day long and served alongside most entrees.

Marinade:
½ C. soy sauce
½ C. orange juice
1 tsp ginger

Pork Tenderloin:
2 pork tenderloins, sliced ½" thick
1 C. soy sauce
½ C. orange juice
1 Tbsp honey
1 orange, diced
1 Tbsp cornstarch
1 Tbsp water
Salt & pepper to taste

Marinade:
1. Mix all ingredients and marinate pork for approximately 45 minutes.

Pork Tenderloin:
1. Mix soy sauce, orange juice and honey in a saucepan. Slowly heat to near boiling.

2. Mix corn starch and water, and add to sauce, stirring to combine.

3. Remove from heat. Add diced orange and season with salt & pepper.

4. In a medium skillet on high heat, sear the pork medallions for 1 minute on both sides.

5. Remove from skillet and arrange on a sizzle (heat proof) plate.

6. Pour sauce over the medallions and place under broiler oven for 3 minutes.

This makes a wonderful dish with jasmine rice or potato of choice. Serves 4-5

THE OLD POST OFFICE RESTAURANT
1442 HWY 174, EDISTO ISLAND

The Old Post Office Restaurant is "deliciously simple with an ambience that is island casual and unobtrusively elegant".

GRILLED FILET MIGNON WITH FRESH GRILLED SHRIMP

Inspired by the everyday family cooking that we grew up with, you'll feel at home while savoring a great meal in our casual and relaxed dining room. Experience our inventive cuisine, attentive service and a friendly atmosphere. Come see what makes us one of the most popular restaurants in town.

Filet Mignon:
Filet mignon
Favorite seasoning

Grilled Shrimp:
16-20 shrimp, peeled & deveined
Old Bay seasoning
2 Tbsp butter

Filet Mignon:
1. Season both sides of filet with your favorite seasoning.

2. Place filet over high heat for 2 minutes to sear and then turn and sear the other side.

3. Reduce to medium heat and cook to desired temperature.

Grilled Shrimp:
1. Season with Old Bay and toss in melted butter.

2. Place on grill and cook for 3-4 minutes on each side.

Follow by a Greek salad, a glass of Merlot and our signature dessert tuxedo chocolate mousse.

OLD TOWN BISTRO
135 E. MAIN STREET, ROCK HILL

"My favorite animal is steak."
Fran Lebowitz, journalist

167

COLLARD GREENS

Chef Orchid Paulmeier runs her kitchen like she lives her life – surrounded by family, friends and feel-good food. Blending time-tested Southern favorites like collards, cornbread and slow-cooked barbecue with her own homespun recipes, One Hot Mama's serves up "comfort food with a kick." Nothing too formal or fancy. Just a warm welcome and good food with a little bit of attitude. This family-friendly restaurant offers delicious baby-back ribs, authentic pit-to-plate BBQ, hand-cut steaks, char-grilled chicken, the world's best wings, salads and more.

1 bag collard greens (approx. 1 ½ lb picked & cleaned)
1 gallon water
1 smoked ham hock
2 Tbsp chicken base
½ C. cider vinegar
1 tsp red pepper flakes
½ C. sugar

1. Bring water, ham hock, chicken base, cider vinegar and pepper flakes to a boil.

2. Add collard greens to boiling water.

3. Sprinkle sugar on top of greens and immerse greens until all greens are covered completely by broth. Bring back to a boil.

4. Reduce to a simmer for 30-40 minutes, until tender.

5. Pull meat from ham hock and throw out bone.

6. Serve with a side of pepper vinegar.

ONE HOT MAMA'S

7 GREENWOOD DRIVE, HILTON HEAD ISLAND

"Vinegar, the son of wine."
Proverb

169

PALMETTO CHEESE STUFFED DEVILED EGGS

If you enjoy pimento cheese and you think you've had the best, we invite you to try our version of pimento cheese made with real sharp cheddar cheese...we call it Palmetto Cheese™. Born in the low country of South Carolina, this pimento cheese has the perfect dipping texture, a smooth taste, and is pleasing to the palate long after the last dip. The recipe originated with Sassy Henry. A family friend and cook, Vertrella Brown of Pawleys Island, is pictured on the container lid as Vertrella is credited with adding the "soulful" touch to Sassy's recipe. The result? Palmetto Cheese™ – The Pimento Cheese with Soul.

6 Tbsp Palmetto Cheese™ Original, Jalapeno or Bacon
6 eggs, hard boiled
¼ C. mayo
Salt & pepper to taste
Paprika

1. Cut hard boiled eggs in half, remove yolks and place into a bowl. Place egg whites onto a serving dish.

2. Mash yolks with a fork until fine. Add mayo and mix until incorporated.

3. Add Palmetto Cheese™ and mix until thoroughly incorporated together.

4. Scoop mixture into a pastry bag or gallon-size food storage bag with one small corner cut off.

5. Pipe mixture onto egg whites. Garnish with a little southern sprinkle of paprika. Enjoy!

Variations: Add finely chopped olives, jalapenos or bacon to give your eggs an added flavor.

"Age is something that doesn't matter, unless you are a cheese."
Luis Buñuel

TEGA HILLS FARM STUFFED ZUCCHINI BLOSSOMS

We love life and food. The belief is a life lived fully is one of Passion. We're dedicated to creating an atmosphere that is both inviting and romantic in which to dwell on what is really essential. Love, music, drink, and food abound with a devotion to exceptional quality. Much of the produce we select is grown locally in keeping with our vision to emulate the great European tradition of hospitality – both on the plate and in the glass. Our romantic hideaway will have you transported to a different time and place. This is where you belong. You're amongst friends…benvenuto. Come experience the rhythm and flavors of Passion8 Bistro where life becomes a little slower with each delectable bite.

Corn & Thyme Veloute:
6 ears of corn, cleaned of husk & silks
1 large onion
4 slices local bacon
2 oz. butter
1 C. heavy cream
Water (as needed)
Salt, pepper & thyme sprigs to taste

Stuffing:
1 C. whole milk
1 C. water or stock
½ C. Anson Mills stone ground grits
3 Tbsp unsalted butter
1 C. parmigiano cheese or local sharp cheese
½ lb white shrimp, peeled & deveined
½ large onion
¼ C. parsley, chopped
2 cloves garlic
2 links of Peach Stand sweet Italian sausage
5 Tbsp white wine
Zucchini blossoms
Kosher salt & pepper to taste

Tempura Batter:
2 C. all-purpose flour
1 large farm egg
1 Tbsp baking powder
2 tsp kosher salt
1 ½ C. sparkling water
Canola oil as needed

Corn & Thyme Veloute:
1. Clean kernels off the cobs and reserve both. Small dice the onion and local bacon. In a stock pot, add butter, bacon, onion and sweat over a medium heat. Add the corn kernels and continue to sweat until onions are translucent. Pour in water to cover 2" above the corn mixture. Add the corn cobs and simmer for 15 minutes. Remove the cobs, add the cream and reduce for 5 minutes on medium heat. Add the thyme and season with salt & pepper. Let cook 10 minutes then ladle mixture into a blender and puree until smooth.

Stuffing:
1. Bring milk and water (or stock) to a boil. Add the grits and whisk immediately to avoid lumps. Cook on low heat approximately 25-30 minutes, continuously stirring. Remove from heat and add the cheese, butter, salt & pepper. Set aside. Rinse and finely chop the shrimp. Remove sausage from casing and sauté in small pieces until brown. Small dice the onion and garlic. Add to sausage and cook until translucent. Add chopped shrimp, parsley, salt & pepper then deglaze the pan with white wine. Mix the shrimp mixture with the grits and allow to cool for 10 minutes. Stuff the zucchini blossoms with shrimp and grits. Twist the ends of each petal to seal stuffing.

Tempura Batter:
1. In a heavy stock pot, heat the canola oil to 350°F. Use enough oil to completely submerge your blossoms. Sift the flour, baking powder and salt in a bowl. Add the whole egg and sparkling water. Whisk to combine. Strain the batter through a sieve (or fine strainer). Dip each zucchini blossom into batter one at a time and allow excess to drip off. Carefully drop each blossom until they are golden brown and crispy. When the blossoms are ready, sprinkle with kosher salt and serve over veloute…oh and enjoy! Serves 6-8.

"Speriamo che tu viva sempre con passione!"
(We hope that you live with passion!)
Luca & Jessica Annunziata, Owners

BAKED OYSTERS ROCKEFELLER

2 slices bacon
24 unopened, fresh, live medium oysters
1 ½ C. cooked spinach
1/3 C. bread crumbs
¼ C. chopped green onions
1 tbsp. chopped fresh parsley
½ tsp. salt
1 dash hot pepper sauce
3 tbsp. extra virgin olive oil
1 tsp. anise flavored liqueur
4 C. kosher salt

1. Preheat oven to 450 degrees F (220 degrees C). Place bacon in a large, deep skillet. Cook over medium high heat until evenly brown. Drain, crumble and set aside.
2. Clean oysters and place in a large stockpot. Pour in enough water to cover oysters; bring the water and oysters to a boil. Remove from heat and drain and cool oysters. When cooled break the top shell off of each oyster.
3. Using a food processor, chop the bacon, spinach, bread crumbs, green onions, and parsley. Add the salt, hot sauce, olive oil and anise-flavored liqueur and process until finely chopped but not pureed, about 10 seconds.
4. Arrange the oysters in their half shells on a pan with kosher salt. Spoon some of the spinach mixture on each oyster. Bake 10 minutes until cooked through, then change the oven's setting to broil and broil until browned on top. Serve hot.

Signature Tastes of SOUTH CAROLINA

PEARLZ OYSTER BAR
CHARLESTON COLUMBIA WEST ASHLEY

"Get action. Seize the moment. Man was never intended to become an oyster."
Theodore Roosevelt

THE BLACK CAT BURGER

Welcome to Poe's Tavern, located two blocks from the beach on Sullivan's Island. Named in honor of Edgar Allan Poe, we're best known for great burgers and drinks. Much like his work, the life of Edgar Allan Poe was short, tragic and shrouded in mystery. Best known as the author of the popular poem "The Raven", Poe is credited with creating the detective and horror story genres. After a brief stint at the University of Virginia, Poe enlisted in the army under the pseudonym Edgar Allan Perry and was stationed at Fort Moultrie at the western end of Sullivan's Island for thirteen months beginning November 18, 1827. His time on the island inspired "The Gold Bug", a story about a mystical beetle that led to buried treasure. He died alone, impoverished and inebriated at the age of 40 amid conflicting accounts of his demise, yet left an indelible legacy on American literature.

Edgar's Drunken Chili:
1 lb ground beef,
browned & drained
1 each green & yellow
bell pepper, diced
1 yellow onion, diced
1 can stewed tomatoes
2 cans black beans,
drained & rinsed
1 Yuengling beer
2 Tbsp garlic, chopped
Chili powder, paprika,
cumin, cayenne, black
pepper & salt to taste

Home Made Pimento
Cheese:
4 oz. cheddar cheese,
shredded
4 oz. Monterey jack
cheese, shredded
4 oz. ricotta cheese
2 oz. mayo
2 oz. green onions,
chopped
3 oz. roasted red bell
peppers, pureed
Salt & pepper to taste

The Burger:
1. Start by grilling 8 oz. of freshly ground 70/30 chuck to your liking. Serve on a freshly baked bun with lettuce, tomato and pickles. Top with 2 slices of apple wood smoked bacon, grilled onions, Edgar's Drunken Chili and Home Made Pimento Cheese.

Edgar's Drunken Chili:
1. Brown the ground beef in a large pot. Remove from heat, strain grease and hold beef to the side.
2. Sweat the onions and peppers with the garlic until translucent. Add the beef, beans, tomatoes, beer and spices.
3. Bring to a low slow simmer for 45 minutes.

Home Made Pimento Cheese:
1. Combine all ingredients in a bowl and mix. For looser consistency add more ricotta; for thicker consistency use less ricotta cheese.

"Deep into that darkness peering, long I stood there, wondering, fearing, doubting, dreaming dreams no mortal ever dared to dream before."
Edgar Allan Poe

PAN SEARED FARM-RAISED SCALLOPS

We're located across from Moss Justice Center (Highway Five) in York, conveniently located half-way between Miami and New York City. Chef Jason Pope, his father Jim Pope, and his uncle Tommy Pope have designed a menu focusing on old time favorites, as well as healthy dishes. At Popes at the White House, every dish is prepared with top quality products, extra large portions and prepared to your order. Our fun and tasty menu makes us your home away from home.

Budero Seasoning:
1 oz. onion powder
2 oz. coriander
2 oz. celery seed
1 oz. granulated garlic
1 tsp cayenne pepper
1 tsp chili powder
1 oz. ginger powder
1 oz. salt
1 oz. pepper
8 oz. pancetta, diced

Grits:
¾ C. Quaker quick grits
4 C. water
2 oz. butter
1 tsp salt
1 tsp white pepper
6 oz. pepper jack cheese, shredded

Scallops:
8 sea scallops, U-10*
3 Tbsp Budero seasoning
¼ C. white wine
1 C. heavy cream
Oil
Cayenne pepper to taste
Salt & pepper to taste

Budero Seasoning:
1. Place all ingredients in a re-sealable bag. Seal and mix thoroughly. Place seasoning on plate to use for the scallops.

Grits:
1. Bring water, butter and salt & pepper to a boil in a 4-quart heavy saucepan and stir in grits. Return to a boil, stirring frequently. Reduce heat and simmer grits, uncovered, stirring occasionally, until thick and most of water is absorbed, about 10-15 minutes. Stir in pepper jack cheese and mix thoroughly. Set aside and keep warm until ready to use. If grits become too thick, stir in water ¼ C. at a time.

Scallops:
1. Heat a large skillet over medium to medium-high heat. Add seasoned pancetta and cook until crispy. Remove from the pan and set aside on paper towels to soak up the oil, but keep warm.
2. Deglaze the pan with the white wine. Slowly add the cream and let reduce until thickened. Season with salt, pepper & cayenne pepper. Add the pancetta mixture back to the sauce.
3. Heat another sauté pan over medium-high heat. When the pan is hot, add oil. Coat each scallop with the seasoning and place in skillet. Cook for 1-2 minutes on each side. DO NOT OVERCOOK!

To serve: Using a 6x6" square plate, place a small amount of grits in the center of the plate. Spoon 1 oz. of pancetta mixture onto the center of the grits. Lay the scallops around the grits in each corner, and then garnish each scallop with a small amount of the mixture. Garnish and serve hot.
Serves 2-4

*Scallops may be sliced horizontally in half if the scallop portion is too large

"Do not overcook this dish. Most seafood...should be simply threatened with heat and then celebrated with joy."
Jeff Smith, 'The Frugal Gourmet'

Okra Blue Crab Fritters

Named after Blackbeard's famous ship, Queen Anne's Revenge serves up premium steaks and seafood in a relaxed atmosphere and is filled with one of the largest collections of authentic pirate artifacts in the country. A pirate lover's paradise, we provide an experience unlike any other on the Carolina coast. Surrounded by authentic artifacts and a tangible history of times when Blackbeard and Calico Jack ruled the oceans, diners feel as if they've been transported through time while enjoying a unique dining experience.

1 lb blue crabmeat, cleaned of shells
3 Tbsp butter
2 Tbsp bacon fat
1 Tbsp salt
½ tsp baking powder
½ tsp baking soda
1 farm egg
2 ½ C. buttermilk
½ C. all-purpose flour
2 C. yellow cornmeal
1 C. okra, sliced

1. Using a wire whisk, mix all ingredients in a large mixing bowl except for crabmeat. The batter should be completely smooth (no cornmeal lumps).

2. Fold in crabmeat using rubber spatula.

3. Fry small scoops of batter in 350°F oil for 1-2 minutes.

4. Serve immediately with remoulade or your favorite dipping sauce.

Queen Anne's Revenge
160 Fairfield Street, Daniel Island

"I don't like gourmet cooking or 'this' cooking or 'that' cooking. I like good cooking."
James Beard

181

Ray's Oak Smoked Pit BBQ

Ray Gaithers is the proud proprietor of Ray's Rib King and he certainly has the name right. Ray turns out what some of our most experienced judges consider to be the best ribs in the state. Then there is the barbeque. It's top notch. Indeed, Ray's is a relatively new barbeque house but it came onto the barbeque scene as a 100 mile barbeque the first time he opened his doors. Ray is a talented man.

4 4-5 lbs Boston butts
14 oz. Ray's Rub, or the rub of your choice
Vinegar
Red oak wood (any oak will do)
Ray's BBQ Sauce, or the sauce of your choice

1. One hour before cooking time, rub butts with rub thoroughly on all sides and place in refrigerator. If meat is going to be used for pulled pork, you may want to cut each butt in 5 pieces as this expedites cooking time and allows more smoke area.

2. With meat in refrigerator, start a fire in the fire box. Allow fire to burn to heat up grill to approximately 200°F.

3. When grill has reached desired temperature, place meat on grill and keep small fire going (just for smoke) in the fire box.

4. If possible never turn meat (some shifting might be necessary). Now sit back and let time do its thing – just be sure to keep the fire box smoking!

5. If the butts were cut, cook 5-6 hours. If cooking whole, cook 10-14 hours.

6. When the seasoning connects with the flavor of the oak, then Ray's Famous BBQ is in the making.

7. Put butts in pan and shred to your liking.

RAY'S RIB KING
4 CASTLE HALL ROAD, YEMASSEE

"Grilling takes the formality out of entertaining. Everyone wants to get involved."
Bobby Flay

183

Red Fish specializes in cuisine where a blend of house made spices, tropical fruits and vegetables are combined with Lowcountry specialties. We're committed to serving our guests the freshest ingredients possible. We have an extensive wine list and diners may also browse the on-site wine shop which boasts more than 1,000 bottles to choose from. Executive Chef, Sean Walsh, has built a unique and intriguing style with combinations of many culinary techniques. At Red Fish, you can expect delectable dishes that express a fusion of the Caribbean and pan-Asian flair brought to traditional Lowcountry cuisine.

Signature Tastes of SOUTH CAROLINA

Udon Noodles:
1 lb Udon noodles
2 oz. brown sugar
½ C. soy sauce
¼ C. rice wine vinegar
1 Tbsp sesame oil
¼ C. sweet thai chili sauce
1 tsp sriracha hot chili sauce
1 tsp ginger, chopped
1 tsp garlic, chopped
1 tsp lemon grass, chopped
1 Tbsp lemon juice

Sea Bass:
Sea bass, cut into 8 oz. portions
Salt & pepper to taste
1 oz. oil
Soy glaze
Wasabi sauce

Udon Noodles:
1. Boil noodles to al dente, strain and leave hot.

2. Combine all other ingredients in a bowl. Add hot noodles and set aside.

3. When the noodles soak up all the sauce, they are ready to eat.

Sea Bass:
1. Season each 8 oz. sea bass portion with salt & pepper.

2. Heat up a sauté pan and add oil. Sear the fish to a golden brown on both sides.

3. When the sea bass is crispy on both sides allow it to finish in a 350°F oven until desired texture and doneness. Cook time is approximately 10-15 minutes.

4. When the fish is done, set aside, and then place Udon noodles in the center of a plate. Place the fish on top of the noodles, drizzle with soy glaze and wasabi sauce.

For additional flavor and garnish, add black sesame seeds, ginger relish and wakame salad.

8 ARCHER ROAD, HILTON HEAD ISLAND

RED FISH

"Don't tell fish stories where the people know you; but particularly, don't tell them where they know the fish."
Mark Twain

PEANUT BUTTER PARFAIT, CHOCOLATE BROWNIE & BUTTERSCOTCH

The South's finest hospitality awaits you at The Willcox. Walk the shady, oak-vaulted streets past clapboard cottages and rambling mansions, and you'll come upon The Willcox, a grand white-pillared glory as lovely and genteel as a rose on a lapel.

Signature Tastes of SOUTH CAROLINA

THE RESTAURANT AT THE WILLCOX
100 COLLETON AVENUE, AIKEN

Chocolate Brownie:
125g dark chocolate (70% cocoa)
125g unsalted butter
2 eggs
150g sugar
40g cocoa
40g flour

Peanut Butter Parfait:
200g sugar
40ml water
10 egg yolks
800ml cream
300g unsalted peanut butter

Butterscotch:
150g brown sugar
200ml cream
150g unsalted butter, chopped

Chocolate Brownie:
1. Preheat oven to 180°C. Melt chocolate and butter in a bowl over a pot of simmering water. Whisk eggs and sugar together until they turn pale. Add cocoa and flour, mix till fully combined. Stir in melted chocolate and pour onto a baking tray lined with a silpat mat. Bake for 8 minutes. Remove and while the brownie is still warm, place a metal rectangular mould, (40cm x 10cm x 10cm) over the brownie and press down so the base of the mould is completely filled. Allow to cool.

Peanut Butter Parfait:
1. Combine sugar and water in a small saucepan, place over high heat and boil until sugar reaches 118°C as measured on a sugar thermometer. Remove from heat and cool for 1 minute. Place egg yolks in an electric mixer and beat together on high speed. Slowly add the syrup in a steady stream and continue beating until egg yolks increase in volume and are thick in consistency. Place the egg yolks in a clean container. Wash the mixing bowl, dry well, then add the cream and beat until the cream just starts to thicken. Add peanut butter and beat till combined. Gently fold in the egg yolk mixture and then pour into the mould on top of the brownie layer. Place in freezer and set overnight.

Butterscotch:
1. Place sugar in a heavy based saucepan with a splash of water and dissolve over high heat until the sugar has caramelized. Add cream and whisk till sauce is smooth. Remove from heat and whisk in butter, piece by piece, until the butter is fully incorporated. Once cooled, carefully pour 200ml of butterscotch over the peanut butter parfait in a thin layer and return to the freezer to set (at least 2 hours).

To Serve: Using a blowtorch, gently warm the sides of the mould and carefully lift off. Slice the parfait with a hot knife, drizzle a plate with butterscotch and place a piece of parfait on top. Serves 12

"I can't walk by chocolate without eating it."
Malin Akerman, Actress

Wild Alaskan King Salmon & Summer Risotto

Deep mahogany wood…warm, subtle lighting…soulful jazz music…the delicate clinking of wine glasses…the soft murmur of voices…heartfelt laughter…this is the mix of sensations and ambiance that creates the wholly unique and inviting atmosphere at Rick Erwin's West End Grille. No detail is too small for Rick when it comes to ensuring the complete satisfaction of his guests. Our menu is based on a tradition of classic steak and fresh seafood. Delight your palate with our signature dishes - Prime and Certified Angus steak aged to Rick's specific requirements and then broiled and perfectly seasoned, making them the most flavorful and tender steaks in Greenville. For those interested in lighter fare, we're proud to offer an array of seafood, all arriving fresh each day. Savor the taste of local, organic fruits and vegetables in our salads and vegetarian dishes. Even our croutons are homemade! Top off your evening with a delicious dessert, such as the world-famous Carnegie Deli Cheesecake, direct from Manhattan.

Signature Tastes of SOUTH CAROLINA

RICK ERWIN'S WEST END GRILLE
648 S. MAIN STREET, GREENVILLE

Risotto:
4 ½ C. stock or water
2 Tbsp butter
1 C. onion, minced
1 clove garlic, minced
¾ C. uncooked Arborio rice
3 Tbsp white wine
1 medium tomato, peeled, seeded & chopped
1 1/3 C. fresh corn kernels
2 C. lima beans
1 red pepper, diced
2 C. fresh peaches
½ C. parmesan cheese, grated
½ C. fresh chives, minced
½ tsp salt
Black pepper to taste

Salmon:
4 8 oz. Wild Alaskan King Salmon filets
1 tsp butter or oil
Salt & pepper to taste

Risotto:
1. In a saucepan, heat stock and keep warm over low heat.
2. Melt butter in a large casserole or in a medium sized pot. Add onions and cook for 4 minutes, stirring occasionally.
3. Add the garlic and rice, stirring constantly for 1 minute.
4. Add the wine and stir till completely absorbed.
5. Using only half, begin to add stock ½ cup at a time, stirring frequently. Wait until stock is almost completely absorbed before adding the next.
6. When the rice has cooked for 15 minutes, add corn, lima beans, tomatoes and red peppers.
7. The risotto should take 18-20 minutes to cook. Season to taste with salt & pepper.
8. Add parmesan, peaches and chives.

Salmon:
1. Season salmon with salt & pepper to preference. In a small skillet or sauté pan, melt butter or oil.
2. Sear salmon for 2-3 minutes on each side till golden brown. Finish cooking in a 350°F oven till desired temperature.
3. Remove salmon from oven and serve on a bed of summer risotto.

"Today our customers are looking for more than a great meal. They want the ultimate dining experience — delicious food, fine wines and exotic cocktails, romantic atmosphere, intimate conversation, stimulating music. That's what they expect — and that's what we strive to give them every time they come to Rick Erwin's."
Rick Erwin, Owner

189

Blackened Tuna Nachos with Watermelon Pico De Gallo

Offering lunch, dinner and a weekend brunch, we invite you to join us in our casual beach restaurant. Chef Anthony DiBernardo is sure to provide something to please with one of his delicious burgers, sandwiches, salads or fresh catch daily specials. We offer live music most nights and have indoor & outdoor seating with TV's all over the place for you to catch your favorite games.

Nachos:
Tortilla chips
Prepared queso
cheese sauce
4 oz. fresh tuna, diced
1 bell pepper, julienned
1 yellow onion,
julienned
¼ C. cooked
black beans
1 jalapeno, sliced
2 Tbsp cilantro,
chopped
6 oz. Monterey jack
cheese, shredded

Pico De Gallo:
1 C. watermelon, diced
¼ C. red onion, diced
1 lime, juiced
1 tsp Cajun seasoning

Nachos:
1. Sauté peppers, onions, jalapenos and black beans.

2. Toss tuna with Cajun seasoning and add to pan.

3. Arrange chips on sheet pan, cover with queso cheese sauce and ingredients from the pan.

4. Cover with shredded jack cheese and ½ of the cilantro.

5. Place under broiler until melted.

Pico De Gallo:
1. Combine watermelon, red onion, remaining cilantro and lime juice.

2. Place on top of nachos before serving.

Serves 2

Rita's Seaside Grille
2 Center Street, Folly Beach

"Is this chicken, what I have, or is this fish? I know it's tuna, but it says 'Chicken of the Sea.'"
Jessica Simpson

ALMOND TOFFEE

Welcome to River Street Sweets! We're proud to deliver simply the freshest, highest quality, most flavorful candies and confections available. We encourage you to watch the products being made, chat with the cooks on duty and sample the candy. We don't want you leaving one of our stores without feeling that you've really experienced something unique and valuable. From the very beginning, customer satisfaction has been at the forefront of our minds. And it always will be. As a family, we take great pride in providing our customers with only the finest Southern candies. It's a custom we want to extend across generations and into your home. Even as we grow, we won't compromise our standards. It goes against our tradition, and besides, life's just too sweet!

2 C. slivered almonds*
1 ½ C. butter, plus additional to grease pan
2 C. sugar
¼ C. water
3 Tbsp light corn syrup
2 tsp vanilla extract
6 oz. chocolate for topping (optional)

1. Spread slivered almonds on ungreased baking sheet and bake at 325°F for 8-10 minutes. Stir halfway to prevent uneven toasting. Chop almonds slightly and split into 2 equal parts and set to the side.

2. Butter a large baking sheet that has a raised edge to keep hot candy from spilling over the edge.

3. Chop up butter and mix in pot with sugar, water and corn syrup. Mix well. Heat over low heat and stir until butter is melted.

4. Turn up heat and brush insides of pot with water on pastry brush, to prevent crystallization. Stir to keep from burning.

5. At 300°F, as measured on a candy thermometer, remove from the burner. Stir in vanilla extract and 1 cup of almonds.

6. Pour toffee in an even sheet and use spatula to spread. Top with chocolate and remaining almonds. Cool in refrigerator for 10-15 minutes.

*Use more or less to desired taste. Other nuts substitute well.

"Water is the most neglected nutrient in your diet but one of the most vital."
Kelly Barton

Rosso Mussels

Signature Tastes of

ROSSO is an elegantly casual Italian trattoria created by one of the founders of Mr. Friendly's, Gervais & Vine and Solstice Kitchen. The warm, open kitchen features a wood-fired grill and wood-burning oven and the cuisine is simple, rustic and absolutely fantastic. Using local, seasonal products whenever possible, the menu boasts an array of antipasti, fresh pastas, grilled meats and wood-roasted dishes. Our wood-grilled Ribeye Fiorentina with Porcini Bearnaise is among the best steaks in town. The wine list is decidedly Italian with some New World wines with Italian spirit. ROSSO also features a variety of Italian spirits and craft beers, as well. The dining room is rustic, yet modern with rich woods and sleek leather chairs. There are two large communal tables for small groups to get together or for strangers to become friends.

2 lbs cultivated mussels
3 Tbsp unsalted butter
1 Tbsp olive oil
3 Tbsp pancetta or bacon, cooked & crumbled
½ C. fennel bulb, thinly sliced
1 Tbsp garlic, minced
½ C. roasted tomatoes (halved cherry tomatoes are fine)
1/3 C. flat-leaf parsley, chopped
1 C. good white wine (or half wine, half chicken broth)
1 tsp kosher salt
½ tsp freshly ground pepper

1. In a large sauté pan or stock pot, heat half the butter and olive oil over medium heat.

2. Add the garlic, bacon, fennel, tomatoes and salt & pepper and cook for 1-2 minutes.

3. Add the mussels and wine and cook for 2-4 minutes.

4. Add the remaining butter and parsley, allowing the butter to melt into the sauce.

5. Serve in a large bowl with grilled or toasted bread.

ROSSO TRATTORIA
4840 FOREST DRIVE, COLUMBIA

"What will be the death of me are buillabaisses, food spiced with pimiento, shellfish, and a load of exquisite rubbish which I eat in disproportionate quantities."
Emile Zola, French writer

Signature Tastes of SOUTH CAROLINA

Saltus River Grill is a unique and exciting restaurant in historic downtown Beaufort. With a grand view of the Intracoastal Waterway from our Sonoma-style patio or from the expansive full-service bar and dining room, this sizzling contemporary seafood grill combines the atmosphere of a chic Manhattan eatery with the historic charm found only in the South Carolina Lowcountry.

Stewed Tomatoes:
Tomatoes*
1 medium yellow onion, diced
3 ribs celery, diced
2 gloves garlic, crushed & minced
¼ C. red wine vinegar
¼ C. sugar
Kosher salt & pepper
1-2 Tbsp neutral oil, such as canola

Pickled Okra:
1 lb fresh okra
2 C. white wine vinegar
1 C. sugar
1 C. water
2 dried chiles, such as Thai chiles or chipotles
10 whole, dried, black peppercorns
5 cloves garlic, skins removed, smashed
1 Tbsp kosher salt

Shrimp:
1 lb 21/25 count wild caught shrimp, peeled & deveined
1 lb apple wood smoked slab bacon, cut into lardons
Sliced pickled okra
Fresh chives, chopped

Stewed Tomatoes:
1. Heat oil in a medium sauce pot on medium heat. Add onions, celery and a 3 finger pinch (~½ tsp) of kosher salt. Cook until the onions and celery are fragrant and starting to turn translucent, but not browned. Stir in the garlic. Continue to cook for 2-3 minutes. Add tomatoes and let simmer on medium/medium-low (depending on how badly it's sputtering) for approximately 20 minutes. Fresh tomatoes will take a bit longer than canned to reduce. Meanwhile, in a small saucepan over medium heat, combine vinegar and sugar. Whisk to dissolve the sugar and let it come to a simmer. Reduce until it takes on a thin syrup consistency, about 10 minutes. Taste the tomatoes, then add the gastrique and taste again. Season with salt & pepper.

Pickled Okra:
1. Wash okra and trim the woody stems. Stand the okra inside of a Mason jar until you can't fit any more in. Combine the remaining ingredients in a medium sized saucepan, bring to a boil and allow to simmer for about 5 minutes. Pour over the okra and let cool in the jars. You can put the lids and bands on while still hot, but allow to cool on the counter. Can be refrigerated for 1 month. Note: Pickled okra should be started at least 24 hours in advance, or you may be able to find it at a Farmer's Market.

Shrimp:
1. Heat a large sauté pan over medium heat and add the bacon. Stir occasionally and allow the bacon to render some of its fat. It will slowly start to brown. If it's browning too quickly, turn the heat down and add 1-2 Tbsp of water. This will allow the bacon to brown, but not become too crispy. Cook for about 8-10 minutes. Remove bacon from pan to a paper towel with a slotted spoon. Drain all but 2-3 Tbsp of bacon fat from the pan and return to a nice, medium heat. Add the shrimp in a single layer, being careful not to overcrowd the pan. This may need to be done in batches. Sear both sides of the shrimp for about 1 minute. Once seared, add all the shrimp back to the pan and cover with stewed tomatoes. Let it come to a simmer, which will fully cook the shrimp. Using your favorite cooked grits, divide among bowls and top with shrimp and tomatoes. Garnish with bacon, pickled okra slices and chopped chives.

*In the wintertime, 1 16 oz. can San Marzano peeled whole tomatoes, crushed by hand or with a wooden spoon. In the summertime, 5 vine-ripened tomatoes, halved, seeded & diced

SALTUS RIVER GRILL
802 BAY STREET, BEAUFORT

"Preserving was almost a mania with Mrs. Bergson....When there was nothing to preserve, she began to pickle."
Willa Cather, 'Death Comes for the Archbishop'

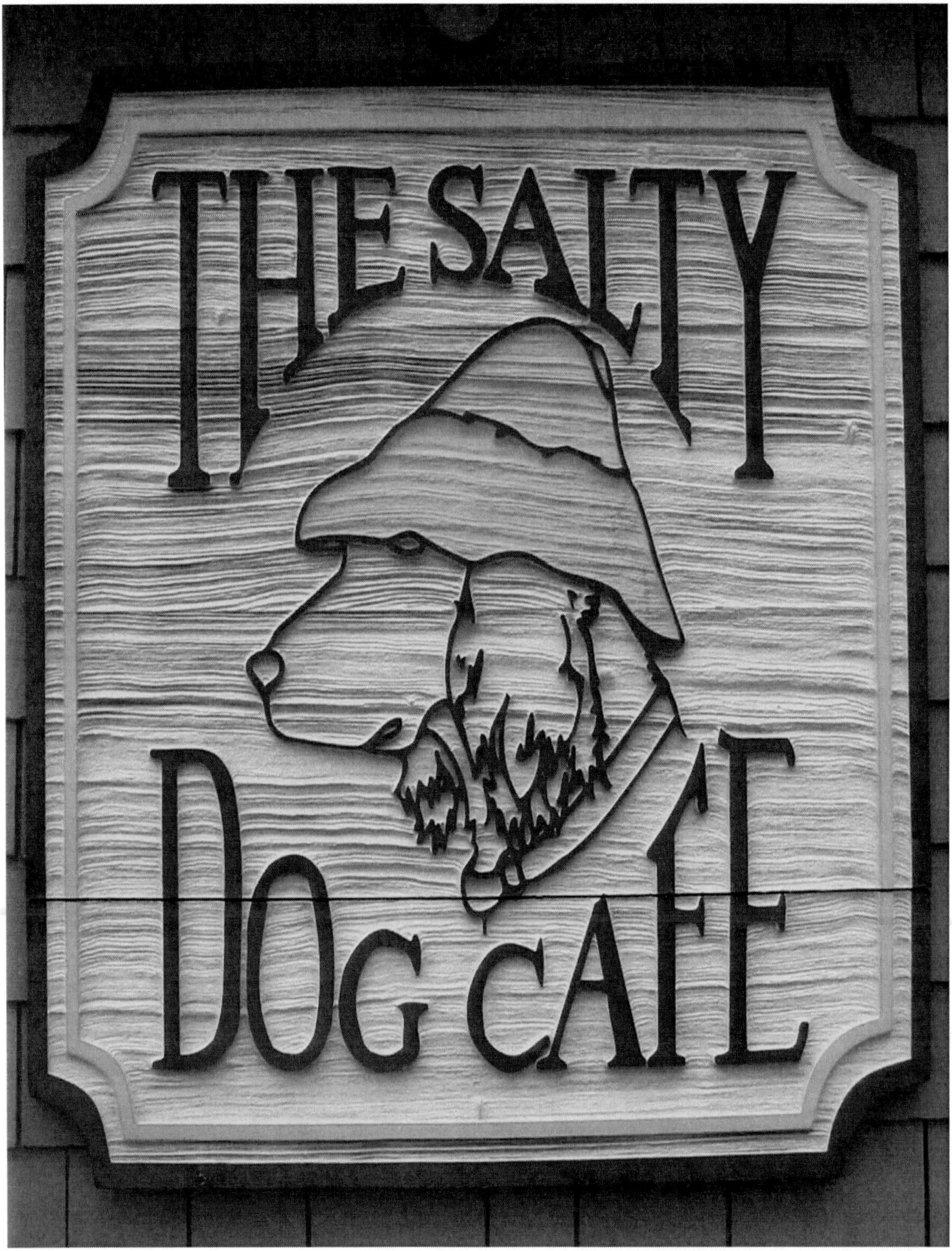
THE SALTY
DOG CAFE

THE SALTY DOG'S KEY LIME PIE

Every year in a fishing village at South Beach, visitors flock to The Salty Dog Cafe located on Hilton Head, a small island just off the coast of America. Some come for the ocean breezes and tropical freezes, while others are seeking a casual atmosphere where both children and adults are entertained. A trip to Hilton Head Island just isn't complete without a visit to The Salty Dog. Enjoy waterfront dining inside at Captain John's Galley where you can order from a full menu of seafood, salads and sandwiches, or enjoy a drink and lighter fare outside on the deck or at the outdoor bar. The night echoes with the tropical sounds of live entertainment. Keep an eye out for the newest Salty Dog, Jake III. The great grandson of the original Jake can often be found wandering the docks in search of some fresh catch or some new friends.

Crust:
½ C. pecans, toasted
2 ½ C. graham cracker crumbs
½ C. butter, melted

Filling:
6 eggs
4 limes, zests of
3 ½ C. sweetened condensed milk
1 - C. Nellie and Joe's Famous Key West Lime Juice

Crust:
1. Toast pecans at 300°F for 5 minutes. Let cool, then puree in food processor.

2. Puree enough graham crackers to make 2 ½ C. crumbs.

3. Mix pecans and graham crackers with melted butter until well combined.

4. Place 2 cups of the pie crust mixture in a lightly greased pie pan. Build up the sides, pressing firmly then add rest of crust to fill out the bottom.

Filling:
1. Mix together all the ingredients until thick and smooth. Place in pie shell and bake at 300°F for 10 minutes.

2. Let cool in the fridge for at least 2 hours before serving.

THE SALTY DOG CAFE
224 S. SEA PINES DRIVE, HILTON HEAD ISLAND

"Almost everything that I behold in this wonderful country bears traces of improvement and reform - everything except Pie.
George Augustus Sala, British journalist. 'America Revisited'

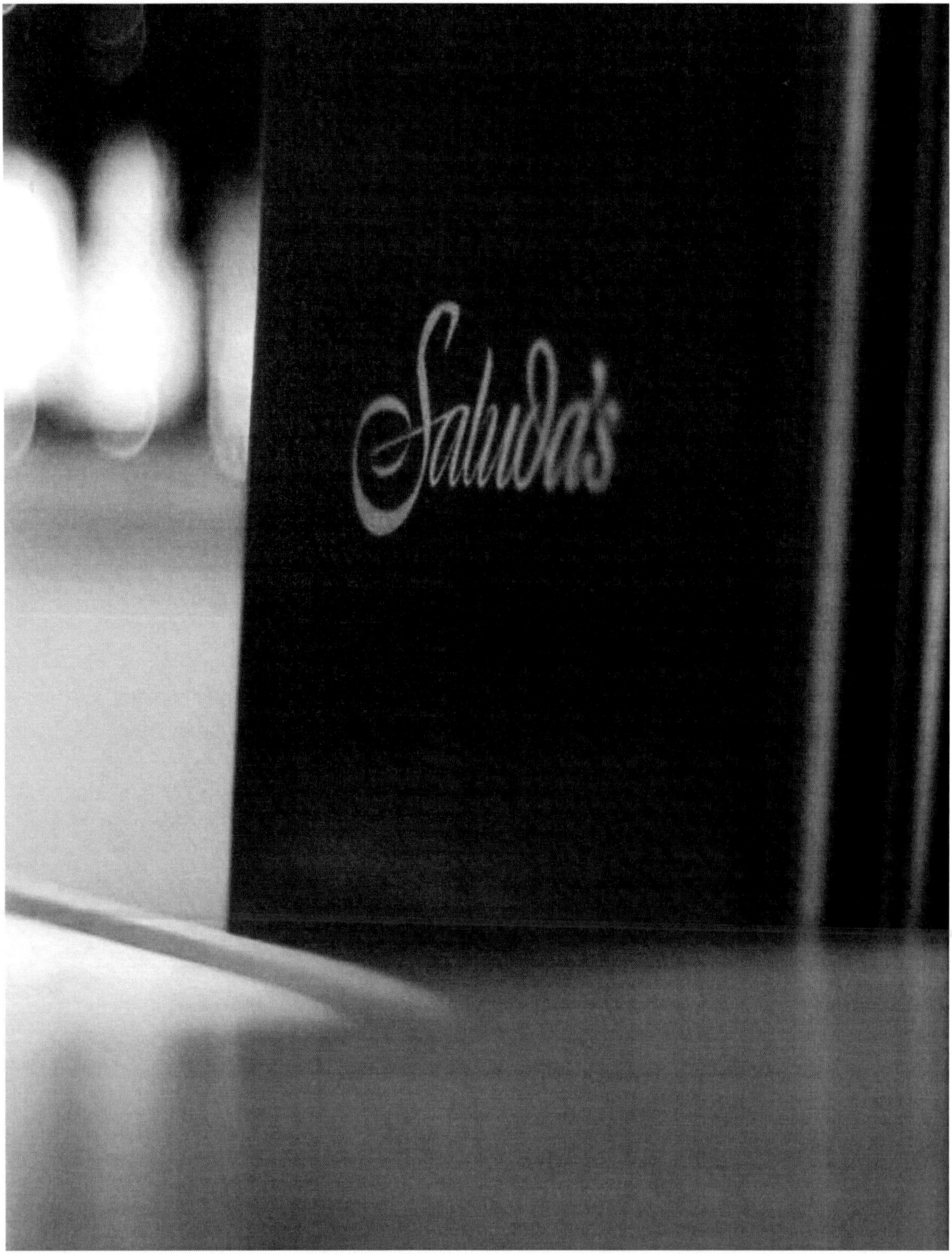
Saluda's

The largest VFW officers club was built at 751 Saluda Avenue after World War I for the specific purpose of entertaining and celebrating on a grand scale. After six years of renovation, the condemned building was reopened in 1996 as Saluda's Restaurant, with nothing less than white linen tables, crystal glassware and a five star executive chef. The solid mahogany bar, an antique from the Blakely Hotel in Philadelphia built in the late 1800's graces Saluda's dining room. Saluda's now exists in the spirit of our veterans celebrations of special occasions. Inspired by local farmers and fishermen, Executive Chef Blake Faries takes fresh SC ingredients and creates classic French and Italian dishes with a Southern flare. With an award-winning wine list and daily specials, Saluda's is the choice for any special evening.

2 ½ lbs shrimp 16/20, peeled & deveined
2 lbs scallops 10/20
1 lb chicken sausage (if not available use Andouille)
1 bunch green onions, sliced on bias
1 pt. grape tomatoes, sliced in half
2 red bell peppers, diced
2 jalapenos, seeds removed & diced
1 yellow onion, peeled & diced
1 - C. Aborio rice
3 ½ C. vegetable broth
2 Tbsp olive oil
½ C. green curry paste
1 pt. heavy cream
1 C. parmesan cheese, shredded
2 limes, juiced
Salt & pepper to taste
Sugar, if necessary

Risotto:
1. Heat vegetable broth to a simmer. Heat oil in sauce pot. Sauté ½ of the onion. Add rice. Cook and stir for 2 minutes Add ½ cup broth and cook until broth is absorbed. Add remaining broth, ½ cup at a time, stirring until all broth is absorbed before adding more. Add ½ cup parmesan cheese. Rice should be creamy and al dente. Season with salt & pepper. Set aside. Total cooking time: 25 minutes.

Green Curry Sauce:
1. Heat oil in sauce pot. Add other ½ of the onion and sauté till soft. Add green curry paste and stir. Paste should become fragrant. Add cream, reduce till sauce like consistency. Add lime juice. If too spicy, add sugar. Salt & pepper to taste. Set aside; keep in warm place.

Sausage:
1. Place whole sausage on a sheet pan and bake at 350°F for 12-15 minutes. Once cooked, cool then slice on a bias.

Jambalaya:
1. Heat enough oil in a large sauté pan to lightly cover the bottom of the pan. Season shrimp and scallops with salt & pepper. When sauté pan starts to lightly smoke, add scallops. After 1 minute scallops should start to brown. Flip the scallops and add shrimp, sausage, red bell peppers, diced jalapenos, halved grape tomatoes and scallions. Add cooked risotto to pan, deglaze with ½ cup vegetable broth and reduce until broth has evaporated. Add ½ cup parmesan cheese. Stir until incorporated. Serves 8.

Pairs well with Staglin Family Salus Chardonnay.

"Fish is meant to tempt as well as nourish, and everything that lives in water is seductive."
Jean-Paul Aron

SCOTT'S SAVORY BBQ SAUCE

Welcome to the one and only world famous Scott's Bar-B-Que! We're located in Hemingway, just a stone's throw from Myrtle Beach. Scott's Bar-B-Que has been serving down home pit-cooked bar-b-que for over 30 years and we love what we do. At Scott's Bar-B-Que, we built our own wood-burning pits to slow cook the whole hog overnight. Come morning, we're ready to sell our mouth watering bar-b-que with a side of skins and our secret family sauce. It doesn't get any better than Scott's Bar-B-Que. Local or long distance, stop by and taste the love.

1 qt. apple cider vinegar
1 (20 ounce) bottle ketchup
¼ C. paprika
1 lb. dark brown sugar
¼ C. salt
1 tbsp. black pepper
2 tbsp. red pepper flakes
1 tbsp. garlic powder
¼ C. Worcestershire sauce
½ C. lemon juice

1. In a large container, mix together the apple cider vinegar, ketchup, paprika, brown sugar, salt, pepper, red pepper flakes, garlic powder, Worcestershire sauce and lemon juice. Pour into an empty vinegar bottle, ketchup bottle or other container and store in the refrigerator for up to 1 month.

2734 HEMINGWAY HWY., HWY. 261 BRUNSON CROSS ROAD, HEMINGWAY

SCOTT'S BAR-B-QUE

"Grilling, broiling, barbecuing - whatever you want to call it - is an art, not just a matter of building a pyre and throwing on a piece of meat as a sacrifice to the gods of the stomach."
James Beard, 'Beard on Food'

SAUTÈED SHRIMP & GRITS WITH REDEYE GRAVY

Second Avenue Pier has the honor and distinction of being the Southern anchor to Myrtle Beach's famous boardwalk. A day on the pier or in the surf can really work up an appetite. Fortunately, great food is just steps away! Our menu features a wide variety of fresh seafood, prepared simply and to order. Large bay windows give diners a million-dollar view. Watch the sun rise over the Atlantic while you sip coffee and prepare for a day at the beach, or enjoy time in our unique open air bar. The wraparound deck features comfy couches and chairs that are great for relaxing and taking advantage of the famous ocean breeze. Whether kicking off a night on the town, or winding down after a day playing in the water, we hope to see you soon here at the Pier!

2 Tbsp olive oil
4 oz. country ham, julienned
¼ C. yellow onions, minced
1 lb medium shrimp, peeled & deveined
1 C. strong coffee
Kosher salt & ground black pepper to taste
1 tsp Tabasco sauce
2 Tbsp butter, cold & cubed
Cooked creamy Stone Ground grits
¼ C. green onions, thinly sliced
1 C. sharp cheddar cheese, grated

1. Heat heavy sauté pan and add olive oil, ham and onions. Stir constantly for 1-2 minutes until onions are translucent.

2. Add shrimp. Keep ingredients moving in pan by stirring or tossing. Turn shrimp after 2 minutes. Shrimp will be pink when ready.

3. Add coffee to the pan and scrape bottom of pan to loosen bits of ham and onions. Reduce coffee by a third.

4. Remove pan from heat and add cubes of butter and Tabasco. Toss or stir pan to distribute evenly. Salt & pepper to taste.

5. To serve, spoon a generous amount of your favorite grits in the bottom of a bowl or pasta dish. Place shrimp on top with gravy and finish with cheese and onions.

Signature Tastes of SOUTH CAROLINA

SECOND AVENUE PIER
110 N. OCEAN BOULEVARD, MYRTLE BEACH

"Food is for eating, and good food is to be enjoyed... I think food is, actually, very beautiful in itself."
Delia Smith, Entertainer

SHRIMP CREOLE

Daily specials at this old roadside store are chalked up on a board; they can include country-fried steak, whole catfish, Jamaican jerk chicken, Buffalo shrimp or oysters (fried in spicy Buffalo-wing style), and fish stew by the cup or bowl. Frying shrimp, scallops, and oysters is a fine art: have a platter or sandwich with very good extra-large French fries and cole slaw on the side.

Signature Tastes of SOUTH CAROLINA

1 55 oz. can whole tomatoes, crushed
1 55 oz. can tomato puree
1 55 oz. can water
8 bell peppers, chopped
6 onions, chopped
1 oz. Old Bay
Salt to taste
3 oz. fresh garlic, chopped
3 lbs shrimp, peeled & deveined

1. Place the whole tomatoes over medium/medium-high heat and boil until tender.

2. Add the tomato puree, water, peppers and onions and reduce heat to simmer for 30 minutes.

3. Add Old Bay, garlic and salt to taste. Cook an additional 30 minutes.

4. Add shrimp and cook 10-15 more minutes, or until shrimp are pink.

5. Serve over fluffy, hot rice.

Serves 20-25

SeeWee Restaurant
4808 Hwy 17 North, Awendaw

"You can even forsake the lowcountry, renounce it for other climates, but you can never completely escape the sensuous, semitropical pull of Charleston and her marshes."
Pat Conroy, **The Prince of Tides**

CAROLINA PIMIENTO CHEESE DIP

We invite you to enjoy a delicious hormone-free, ground-in-house hamburger, sandwich, or salad here at Sesame Burgers & Beer. Starting from the ground up, we make all of our food from scratch. We're a growing local restaurant concept that's given the all American burger a creative, delicious twist. Pairing the usual with the unusual is mainstay here, where the build your own topping options are endless. Try some of our famous house made condiments or bread & butter pickles on your burger, or choose one of our many house made salad dressings. Teaming great food with friendly service, a comfortable atmosphere and a huge selection of beer is a winning combination. We're proud of our products and are sure you'll enjoy our friendly and accommodating staff as much as you enjoy our food.

12 C. sharp cheddar cheese
6 C. parmesan cheese
3 ½ C. mayo
1 bunch parsley, chopped
2 ½ tsp cayenne pepper
5 C. roasted red peppers, diced
2 C. liquid from the peppers

1. Grate all cheese and use canned red peppers reserving the liquid.

2. Mix all ingredients in a large mixing bowl.

3. Serve with warm pita, or put on top of your favorite burger and broil.

4726 SPRUILL AVENUE & 2070 SAM RITTENBURG BOULEVARD, CHARLESTON

SESAME BURGERS & BEER

"Age is of no importance unless you are a cheese."
Billie Burke, Actress

CHOCOLATE-COVERED CHERRY POUND CAKE

SideTracked's name is a double entendre. Not only are we located right beside the railroad tracks, but "sidetracked" careers is how we got into this business in the first place. We serve 6-8 items on our menu, but the entire menu changes weekly. It's a very eclectic selection. On any given week, you might find Wolfgang Puck's Hungarian Goulash as a choice alongside Classic Meatloaf or White Chicken Lasagna. There's always quiche and a specially-seasoned Fried Chicken Breast. Almost everything is homemade from scratch with fresh ingredients. We rotate 16 different soups during the fall and winter months and are famous for our homemade desserts – offering 3 different ones each week just like Grandma used to make! With our continued success, it looks like we might stay SideTracked for a long time.

Pound Cake:
2 sticks butter, room temp
½ C. shortening
3 C. sugar
5 eggs, room temp
1 C. Cherry Crush or other cherry-flavored soft drink
3 C. all-purpose flour
½ tsp salt
1 Tbsp cherry or almond flavor extract

Chocolate Buttercream Icing:
3 sticks butter, room temp
3 C. powdered sugar
- C. cocoa powder
1 tsp cherry or almond flavor extract

Cherry Sauce:
2 cans sweetened condensed milk
1 jar maraschino cherries (reserve syrup)
Red food coloring
1 C. powdered sugar
1 tsp cherry or almond extract

Pound Cake:
1. Preheat oven to 350°F. Grease and flour a bundt or tube pan. Cream together the butter, shortening and sugar until fluffy, about 3 minutes. Add eggs, one at a time, beating well after each addition. In second bowl, sift flour and salt together. Add dry ingredients to butter mixture alternating with cherry soda. Add flavoring extract. Pour batter into pan and bake for about 70 minutes. Cool cake in pan for about 30 minutes before attempting to remove. Remove from pan and let cool completely on wire rack.

Chocolate Buttercream Icing:
1. Cream butter with mixer. In separate bowl, whisk together powdered sugar and cocoa powder. Gradually pour dry ingredients into creamed butter, mixing continuously for smooth consistency. Add flavoring extract and mix well. If icing is too soft, you may refrigerate to firm it back up a bit.

Cherry Sauce:
Mix sweetened condensed milk and powdered sugar together using whisk attachment on mixer. Make sure sugar is thoroughly dissolved into mixture (no lumps). Drain maraschino cherries and pour the syrup into the mixture, retaining cherries to garnish cake. Add flavoring extract. Add 1 or 2 drops of red food coloring if you desire a pinker hue. Serve cherry sauce on the side or use as a drizzle over each slice of cake as it's served. Cake may also be drizzled with chocolate syrup.

SIDETRACKED CAFÉ & CATERING
107 BROAD STREET, CENTRAL

"Let's face it, a nice creamy chocolate cake does a lot for a lot of people; it does for me."
Audrey Hepburn

Signature Tastes of SOUTH CAROLINA

Located on the waterfront of Skull Creek, you'll enjoy beautiful views whether you choose to dine indoors on fresh seafood and American favorites with a twist, at the Dive Bar – a raw bar featuring fresh sushi, oysters and more – or dine outdoors on the terrace. The open-air Buoy Bar serves up colorful sunset views and the freshest original drinks. So bring your family – bring your friends – bring yourself to Skull Creek Boathouse. One bite and you're hooked!

Tasso Gravy:
½ C. green bell peppers, coarse chopped
½ C. yellow onion, coarse chopped
½ C. celery, coarse chopped
1 C. Tasso ham, diced
⅓ C. clarified butter
½ C. flour
1 Tbsp fresh garlic, chopped
¼ C. white wine
⅛ tsp cayenne pepper
1 ¼ qt. chicken stock
⅛ C. fresh thyme
½ Tbsp ground black pepper
½ tsp Tabasco
⅛ tsp white pepper

Grits:
High quality stone ground grits
3 C. chicken stock
¼ tsp white pepper
3 dashes Crystal hot sauce
2 Tbsp butter
¼ C. heavy cream

Shrimp:
32 shrimp 16/20, peeled & deveined
8 oz. Andouille or smoked sausage, large diced
1 C. fresh tomatoes, diced
2 Tbsp butter

Tasso Gravy:
1. Heat butter and flour in thick bottom 6 qt. pot, stirring constantly until mixture (roux) becomes golden brown. Add bell peppers, onions, celery and Tasso Ham, stirring to combine.
2. Cook, stirring regularly for 8-10 minutes or until vegetables are soft. Add white wine, stir and cook 2 minutes. Add the rest of the ingredients and stir. Cook on a simmer for 20 minutes. Let cool and then puree in a food processor.

Grits:
1. Add grits (we use Anson Mills Yellow Organic Stone Ground Grits) and stock to a thick bottom pot. Let grits settle and skim any particles from the top by slightly tilting the pan.
2. Turn on heat, bring to a boil and lower to a simmer, stirring regularly to keep the grits from sticking to the bottom of the pan. Cook for 2 to 2 ½ hours. Grits should be tender but not mushy. Add butter and heavy cream. Set aside and keep hot.

Shrimp:
1. Heat the butter in a large sauté pan and add shrimp and sausage. Cook on high heat 2 minutes. Add tomatoes and cook 2 minutes more. Add 6 cups of the Tasso gravy, heating through.
2. Divide grits into 4 bowls. Top evenly with shrimp and Tasso gravy. Enjoy!

SKULL CREEK BOATHOUSE
397 SQUARE POPE ROAD, HILTON HEAD ISLAND

"I shall be but a shrimp of an author."
Thomas Gray

SLATHERED SHRIMP OVER PIMENTO CHEESE GRITS

Nothing says true Southern more than a Lowcountry shrimp & grits recipe. Entire cookbooks from award winning chefs have been written about this dish with all its variations and cooking methods. Although there is an abundance of amazingly delicious shrimp & grits recipes, I chose to share this one because Slathered Shrimp & Grits is more than delicious ingredients melded together yielding a taste that tantalizes the palette – there is story behind each layer of this recipe. It represents an evolution and culmination of over 100 years of cooking history and draws on my rich family heritage. It is one of my family favorites and one that I am proud to share with you.

Roasted Peppers:
Red bell peppers
Olive oil

Pimento Cheese Grits:
6 C. water
1 ½ C. coarse stone ground yellow grits
4 oz. cream cheese
4 Tbsp butter
8 oz. sharp cheddar cheese
1 C. roasted peppers, chopped
½ Tbsp sea salt
Dash of white pepper

Slathered Shrimp:
1 ½-2 lbs fresh, domestic wild caught shrimp, peeled & deveined
2 Tbsp olive oil
½ - 1 bottle Slather Brand Foods Original Slatherin' Sauce
12 slices premium crispy bacon
¼ C. fresh parsley, chopped

Roasted Peppers:
1. You can use store bought roasted peppers, however I prefer to roast my own. Roasting peppers is very easy to do and can be refrigerated and used for other recipes. Preheat oven to 500°F. Rub washed and dried peppers with olive oil and place on baking sheet in top rack in oven. Roast for about 25-30 minutes turning once or twice until skin is blistered and charred in some places. Remove from oven and place in bowl covered tightly with plastic wrap. Let cool for 10-15 minutes. Peel the skin and then remove stems, cores and seeds.

Pimento Cheese Grits:
1. Bring water to boil in heavy-bottom stockpot. Slowly add grits, stirring constantly. Reduce heat to low and continue stirring to prevent grits from scorching. Once grits have started to thicken, continue cooking over low heat for another 30 minutes, stirring frequently. Add remaining ingredients and continue cooking for about 10 minutes until cheese melts and roasted peppers are well blended. Grits should be very creamy and smooth. If mixture is too thick, simply add water ¼ C. at a time to get desired consistency. Season to taste with salt & pepper. Keep covered and warm until ready to serve adding water as needed to maintain creamy consistency.

Slathered Shrimp:
1. While grits are cooking, place bacon slices on foil lined baking sheet and place in 350°F oven until crispy. Remove from oven, drain on paper towels, crumble and set aside. Place oil in heavy bottom saucepan over medium-high heat. Add shrimp and stir, moving shrimp to sides of the pan. Pour Slatherin' Sauce in the middle of the pan. Sauce will quickly begin to caramelize. Fold the sauce and shrimp together in the pan for about 3 minutes until shrimp are thoroughly cooked but being careful not to overcook.

To serve: Spoon hot pimento cheese grits on plate. Top with heaping spoonful of Slathered Shrimp. Generously sprinkle with bacon crumbles and finish with sprinkled chopped parsley. The colors and smells are beautiful and the taste is amazing, so don't be surprised when your family asks you to "Slather It On" more often! Serves 6.

Signature Tastes of SOUTH CAROLINA

CHEF ROBIN RHEA, OWNER & CREATIVE MASTERMIND
SLATHER BRAND FOODS

"The Slather Brand Foods'™ philosophy is to provide products that we are proud to serve our family, our friends, and just as importantly, our customers."
Chef Robin Rhea

Solstice Kitchen & Wine Bar
presents
"Doughnuts for Amy"
with
author & chef John Malik
March 6, 2012

reception
of La Marca Prosecco & antipasti, cheese &
accompaniments

first course
Grilled Zucchini, shaved tomme cheese, evoo,
roasted red pepper sauce, chives, sea salt, black pepper
-Royal Chenin Blanc, South Africa-

second course
"BLT" Salad, iceberg lettuce, grilled crouton,
smoked cheddar, applewood bacon, Wil-Moore egg,
buttermilk ranch dressing
-Definitive Chardonnay, Napa Valley-

third course
Pan Roasted Duck Breast, pinot noir cherry sauce,
thyme, black pepper, vanilla bean
-Brandborg Pinot Noir, Oregon-

fourth course
Braised Beef Short Rib, truffle oil, parsley,
yukon gold mashed potatoes
-Copain Syrah, Washington-

fifth course
Malted Milk & Vanilla Bean Doughnut,
dark chocolate-espresso glaze
-have some coffee-

Vanilla-Honey Grits Soufflé

Welcome to the kitchen of Solstice! Without a doubt, it's the backbone of the restaurant and ultimately the reason we're all here – we love to eat! But it's not just about eating. It's about cooking. It's about taking the time to ensure things are perfect. It's about offering you an experience you couldn't have dreamed of having. We rely on our numerous purveyors for everything from fish and beef, to vegetables and cheese. Our menu is full of creations that are 100% in-house and we search high, low, left and right for anything and everything to be sure we're offering the best products available. Finally – our menus are designed to reflect what the term Solstice means…the changing of the Seasons. While it would be easier to simply offer easier-to-find, more traditional items, we must keep ourselves entertained and therefore change our menu in some way, shape or form, every single day. So whether you come in expecting to get what you had last time, or you're adventurous enough to try something different every time, please understand our plight. We are what we cook. And we are different from season-to-season, from day-to-day and from week-to-week.

2 C. vegetable stock plus 1 C. water (you can use 3 C. water instead)
2 tsp salt
1 C. white grits
1 C. heavy cream
5 eggs, separated
¼ C. honey
1 tsp vanilla extract
¼ C. brown sugar
2 tsp sugar
4 Tbsp unsalted butter
Salt & coarsely ground black pepper to taste

1. Butter a 2 qt. casserole or soufflé dish; set aside.
2. In a 3 qt., heavy-bottomed saucepan, bring the stock, water and salt to a boil.
3. Stir in the grits, reducing the heat to medium, and cook, stirring often, until thick, smooth and creamy.
4. In a small saucepan, heat the heavy cream until hot, then stir into the grits.
5. Beat the egg yolks then slowly whisk them into the grits.
6. Stir in the honey, vanilla, brown sugar and sugar; season with salt & pepper. Cool at room temperature.
7. An hour before serving the soufflé, preheat oven to 375°F.
8. In a stainless steel bowl, beat the egg whites until they form stiff peaks.
9. Gently fold the egg whites into the grits mixture and spoon into the buttered soufflé dish. Bake 25-30 minutes or until the grits are set. Serve immediately.

Serves 8

"A thriving household depends on the use of seasonal produce and the application of common sense."
Olivier de Serres (1539-1619)

CM

Summer Salsa

4 Lrg Tomatoes, Diced
1 Lrg Yellow or White Onion, Diced
1/4 Yellow Bell Pepper, Diced
1/4 Green Bell Pepper, Diced
1/4 Garlic Clove (Minced)
1/2 cup finely chopped Cilantro
1/2 cup Chopped Green Onions
1 lemon (juice only)
1 tablespoon lime juice
Salt (2 pinches)
Pepper (2 pinches)

Toss all ingredients together in a large bowl and
place in fridge to cool, about 30 minutes. Serve
with fresh baguette slices or with homemade
tortilla chips or pita chips!

TOMATO BREAD PUDDING

RECIPE COURTESY OF BLANCHE WEATHERS

Signature Tastes of **SOUTH CAROLINA**

SOUTH CAROLINA DEPARTMENT OF AGRICULTURE
494 CAMDEN ROAD VANCE

The Certified South Carolina program is a cooperative effort among producers, processors, wholesalers, retailers and the South Carolina Department of Agriculture (SCDA) to brand and promote South Carolina products. Our goal is for consumers to be able to easily identify, find and buy South Carolina products. Fresh on the Menu, the second phase of the Certified SC program, was launched in February 2008 and is a commitment to provide South Carolina citizens the freshest products and produce from some of the nation's best restaurants. Restaurants throughout South Carolina have become partners in the effort. Participating chefs agree to prepare menus that include at least 25% Certified South Carolina Grown foods and products in season and feature the Fresh on the Menu brand. These chefs recognize the value in supporting local for not only their bottom lines, but also for the difference South Carolina local products and produce make on the taste of food. The South Carolina Department of Agriculture challenges all South Carolinians to support, ask for and remember "Locally grown. It's to dine for."

V12 oz. challah bread, diced
1 lb tomatoes, diced
½ lb butter
1 oz. garlic, finely chopped
1 C. heavy cream
Salt & pepper to taste
¼ C. palmetto sweet onions, diced
½ oz. basil chiffonade
6 butter pats

1. Cut bread into 1" cubes and roast in 350°F oven for 7-12 minutes until brown and crunchy.
2. Cut tomatoes into ¾" cubes and set aside.
3. Melt 3 Tbsp butter in large pan, add onion and cook until tender.
4. Add garlic and continue cooking until garlic is golden.
5. Add remaining butter and tomatoes and cook for 7 minutes.
6. Add cream, salt & pepper and bring to a simmer.
7. Add basil and cool for 2 minutes.
8. Place crunchy bread cubes in large bowl. Pour liquid over bread and mix with gentle folding action to thoroughly coat bread. Allow to sit for 15 minutes or refrigerate for several hours.
9. Pour into non-stick pan and place 6 butter pats on top. Place in moderate oven and heat thoroughly.

Buy South Carolina because Nothing's Fresher. Nothing's Finer.

219

PEACHY FRENCH TOAST

On a warm summer day, don't you love to bite into a juicy, sweet, mouth-watering peach? That's just what you get when you choose South Carolina peaches. The Palmetto State's hot days, humid nights, and slightly acidic soils combine to produce the sweetest, juiciest, and best-tasting peaches on the market. Working with Mother Nature, our growers produce tree ripened peaches bursting with juice and flavor. We invite you to learn more about the "Tastier Peach State" and to "Taste the Difference" for yourself.

Signature Tastes of SOUTH CAROLINA

Peaches:
12 large ripe SC peaches
¾ C. sugar
1/3 C. all-purpose flour
Cooking spray

Toast:
¼ C. sugar + 2 Tbsp
1 tsp grated orange rind
1/3 C. fresh orange juice
¼ C. unsalted butter, melted
¼ tsp ground cinnamon
Dash of nutmeg
½ teaspoon vanilla
2 large eggs
12 slices stale French bread, thick cut

Peaches:
1. Carefully cut an X on the bottoms of peaches just through the skin.
2. Add ice water to a large pot. Fill another large pot with water and boil.
3. Dunk the peaches into the boiling water for 20 seconds. Remove with a slotted spoon, and put into ice water.
4. Slip loose skins off peaches. Cut peaches in half, remove pits and slice.
5. Preheat oven to 350°F. Spray a 13" x 9" baking dish with cooking spray.
6. Combine peaches, sugar and flour. Pour into baking dish. Let stand 30 minutes.

Toast:
1. Combine ¼ C. sugar, orange rind, orange juice, butter, cinnamon, nutmeg and eggs.
2. Cut the bread slices into 2 triangles.
3. Dip bread into the orange juice mixture, then arrange on top of peach mixture. Sprinkle 2 Tbsp sugar over bread.
4. Bake at 350°F for 45 minutes or until golden.
Serves 8

SOUTH CAROLINA PEACH COUNCIL
1200 SENATE STREET, COLUMBIA

"We realize consumers have a choice and we thank you for choosing South Carolina peaches."
South Carolina Peach Council

PEACH COBBLER

Judy Brown, Director of Foodservices, was gracious enough to share this tasty treat with us, courtesy of their wonderful little restaurant, Judy's at the Market. The restaurant serves Southern-style comfort foods, sandwiches, hamburgers and hot dogs. Judy studied at the Culinary Institute of Charleston and has had the privilege of attending the culinary school, Aspicius, in Florence, Italy. Judy has taught several pastry and culinary classes and plan to continue teaching classes in the markets state-of-the-art exhibition kitchen in the very near future.

Filling:
3 lbs peaches
2 Tbsp all-purpose flour
2 Tbsp sugar

Topping:
2 C. self-rising flour
2 C. sugar
1 egg
¼ C. pecans, chopped
1 stick butter, melted

1. Preheat oven to 350°F. Peel the peaches, remove the pits and slice.

2. In a medium sized bowl, toss together filling ingredients and pour mixture into a greased 13x9" baking pan.

3. Combine the first 4 topping ingredients (you can use the same bowl that you used to mix the filling) until crumbly.

4. Sprinkle the topping evenly over the peaches and drizzle with melted butter.

5. Bake for about 45-50 minutes or until filling is bubbly and topping is browned.

Signature Tastes of SOUTH CAROLINA

SOUTH CAROLINA STATE FARMERS MARKET
3483 CHARLESTON HWY, WEST COLUMBIA

"Chocolate's okay, but I prefer a really intense fruit taste. You know when a peach is absolutely perfect... it's sublime. I'd like to capture that and then use it in a dessert."
Kathy Mattea, Musician

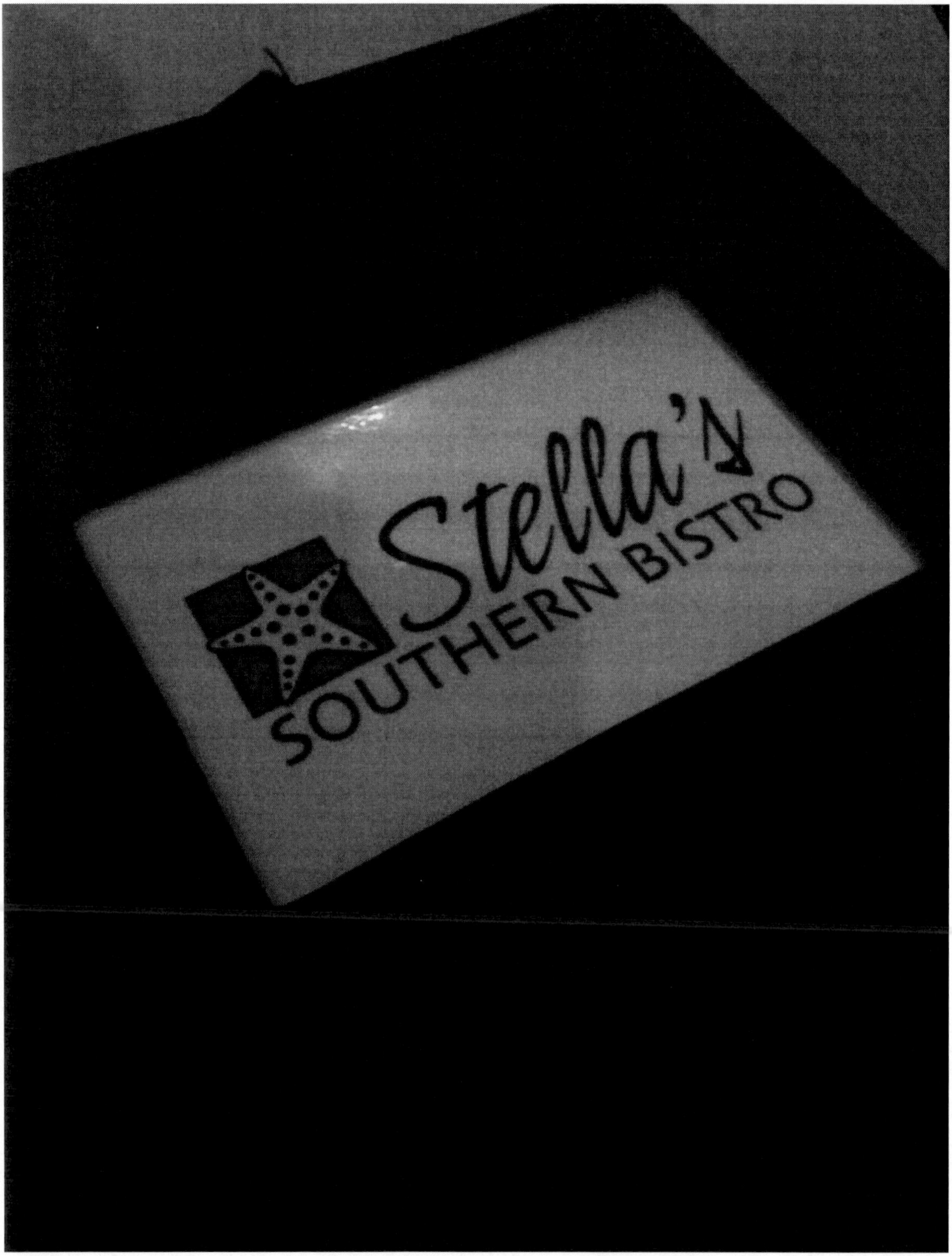
Stella's
SOUTHERN BISTRO

SHRIMP & GRITS

Signature Tastes of

Owners, Jason and Julia Scholz, bring their vision of friendly service and excellent cuisine to Stella's Southern Bistro. We're enthusiastic about sourcing as many local ingredients as we can find and supporting our local farmers. Stella's cuisine is inspired by the coastal Carolinas' and the American South. Serving lunch and dinner, Stella's is a great place to unwind with a signature cocktail at the bar, or dinner in the dining room. Join us for a relaxed atmosphere, great food & genuine hospitality. We're an ideal place for a unique dining experience.

Grits:
1 C. heavy cream
1 C. milk
1 C. water
1 C. stone ground grits
½ lb butter
2 Tbsp salt

Shrimp Stock:
Shrimp shells
3 Tbsp vegetable oil
½ onion, chopped
1 celery stalk, chopped
1 carrot, chopped
1 bay leaf
4 black peppercorns
2-3 sprigs of thyme
1 Tbsp tomato paste
2 C. white wine
6 C. water

Shrimp Ragout:
12 slices (thick) apple wood smoked bacon
1 C. cooked red bell pepper, diced
36 shrimp 21/25, peeled & deveined
2 Tbsp Cajun seasoning
1 C. green onions, sliced
1 ½ C. canned Roma tomatoes, diced
4 Tbsp butter
1 C. shrimp stock

Grits:
1. Bring cream, milk, water and butter to a simmer. Reduce heat to low. Stir in grits and salt and cook for 40 minutes to 1 hour, stirring often to prevent grits from sticking to bottom of pot. Keep warm.

Shrimp Stock:
1. Save shrimp shells in a separate colander while peeling shrimp. In a large pot, heat oil. Add shrimp shells and sauté until they turn pink.
2. Add onion, celery and carrot. Sauté for 1-2 minutes. Add bay leaf, peppercorns, thyme and tomato paste. Mix and sauté an additional 3-5 minutes.
3. Add 1 cup of white wine and stir. Let the wine evaporate. Add another cup, stir and repeat. Add water and let simmer about 10 minutes.
4. Let the mixture cool, then blend and strain with a fine strainer. Shrimp stock will keep in the refrigerator for up to a week.

Shrimp Ragout:
1. Cook bacon at 350°F for 30 minutes, or until the bacon is cooked but not crispy. Slice into ¼" pieces.
2. In a wide (14-16") pan, add shrimp, bacon, tomatoes, Cajun seasoning, peppers and shrimp stock. Cook on medium-high heat until shrimp are nearly cooked, 6-8 minutes. Add butter and ½ of green onions. Stir well and cook until shrimp are done.
3. Divide grits among 6 large deep bowls. Top with 6 shrimp each. Pour remaining mix over top of shrimp then equally scatter remaining green onions for garnish. Serve immediately.

STELLA'S SOUTHERN BISTRO
684-C FAIRVIEW ROAD, SIMPSONVILLE

"If music be the food of love, play on."
William Shakespeare

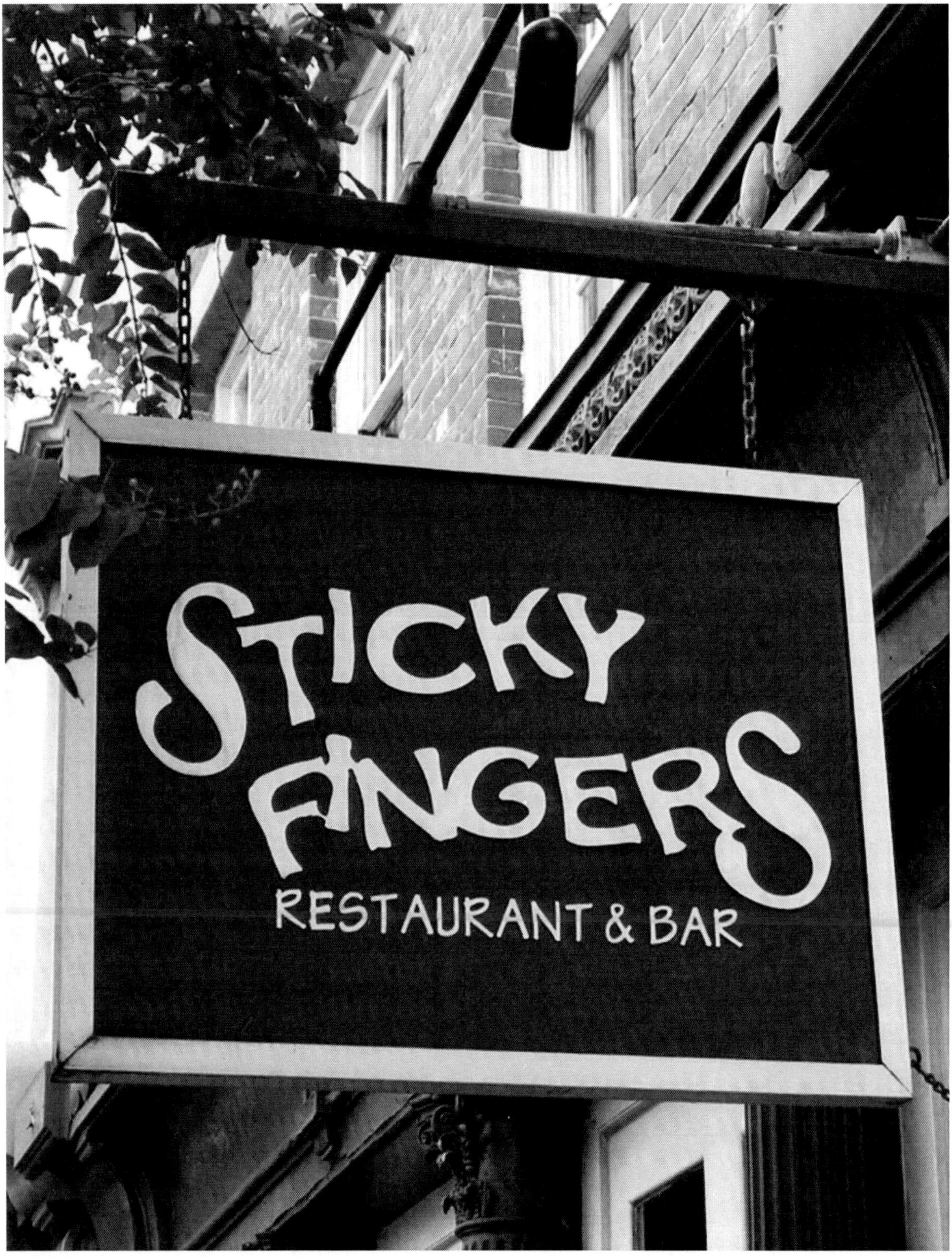
STICKY
FINGERS
RESTAURANT & BAR

RIBS & PULLED PORK SHOULDER

Founded by three lifelong friends, Sticky Fingers opened in Mt. Pleasant in 1992. Armed with little money and even less experience, we set about doing what we knew best: treating our guests the way they wanted to be treated. Since that time, we've established a reputation for serving award winning barbecue in the Southeast – home of the best barbecue in America! With locations in the Carolinas, Tennessee, Georgia and Florida, the sweet smell of hickory wood that welcomes you upon arrival is a sure sign that all of our smoked meats are still slow cooked on-site in our barbecue pits. It's that same commitment to tradition and authenticity that makes our restaurants and signature barbecue sauces so popular.

3 tbsps pimenton
2 tbsp. garlic powder
2 tsp. cayenne
1 tbsp salt
1 tbsp. brown sugar
1 tbsp. celery salt
1 tbsp. dry mustard
1 boston butt (in 7 to 9 lb. boston butt x patterns cut in the fat cap)
1 beer
3 C. apple cider vinegar
2 cloves garlic (smashed)
2 chilies (fresno, sliced in half)
¼ C. brown sugar
¼ C. tomato paste
1 tbsp kosher salt
2 tbsp. dijon mustard
12 toasted buns (burger)

1. Preheat the oven to 225 degrees F.
2. Combine all the spices for the rub and massage it into the meat. Place the rubbed pork in a roasting pan and pour the beer into the pan. Cover it with foil and roast for 6 hours. Check it periodically just to make sure everything is going along just fine, turning it over every 2 hours.
3. Remove the foil and roast until the pork has reached an internal temperature of 190 degrees F, about another 3 hours. Remove it from the oven, cover it loosely with foil, and let it rest for 30 minutes.
4. Sometime during the marathon cook time, make the sauce. In a small saucepan combine all the ingredients and bring to a boil. Taste it to make sure it is delicious. Remove the chiles. When the sauce is cool, I recommend putting it in a squeeze bottle for easy use.
5. Remove the bone from the pork, it should slide right out. Using your hands with dish gloves on, or with two forks, start to "pull" the pork into long shreds. Get rid of the fat and anything else that doesn't look delicious.
6. Serve the pork on burger buns with a drizzle of vinegar sauce to your liking.

"Grilling, broiling, barbecuing – whatever you want to call it – is an art, not just a matter of building a pyre and throwing on a piece of meat as a sacrifice to the gods of the stomach."
James Beard

STUFFED PORK CHOPS

We're located in the heart of downtown Anderson in the historic Sullivan Building, once home to one of the largest hardware stores in the Southeast. Our number one goal is to delight you – our customer – because without you, we're nothing. Dining at our restaurant is like dining in our home. We genuinely care about you and are grateful for every person that walks through our doors. Our cuisine is heavily influenced with Mediterranean flavors, which is a reflection of our Greek heritage. The menu is eclectic with a wide range of flavors and the desserts are the best on the planet! Serving "Bold American Cuisine with a Touch of the Mediterranean"…that's our motto. We'd love the opportunity for you to dine with us.

Signature Tastes of SOUTH CAROLINA

Pork Chops:
2 lbs center cut pork loin
12 oz. goat cheese
2 ½ oz. extra virgin olive oil
2 lemons, juiced
3 cloves garlic
1 oz. fresh basil, chopped
1 Tbsp dried oregano
1 ½ tsp kosher salt
Fresh cracked pepper to taste

Balsamic Caramelized Onion Reduction:
1 medium Spanish onion
1 ½ oz. extra virgin olive oil
4 oz. balsamic vinegar
¼ C. sugar

Balsamic Caramelized Onion Reduction:
1. Peel and thinly slice onion. In a heavy bottom saucepan, add olive oil, sliced onion and "sweat" over medium-low heat for 10-12 minutes.

2. Add balsamic vinegar, sugar and reduce 20-25 minutes, until thick. Hold at room temperature or slightly warm.

Pork Chops:
1. Cut pork loin into 4 oz. chops 1" thick (about 8 chops). With the fat facing outward, cut a 1 ½" long and ¾" deep "pocket" into each chop.

2. Stuff each pocket with approximately 1 ½ oz. of goat cheese.

3. Marinate chops with 2 ½ oz. of olive oil, garlic , lemon juice, basil, oregano, salt & pepper and then refrigerate for 2-3 hours.

4. Heat gas or charcoal grill to medium-high heat and grill chops approximately 7 minutes on each side.

5. Serve on a bed of garlic mashed potatoes.

SULLIVAN'S METROPOLITAN GRILL
208 S. MAIN STREET, ANDERSON

"There is poetry in a pork chop to a hungry man."
Philip Gibbs (NY Times 1951)

229

3 FLAVOR POUND CAKE

Here is our signature pound cake, this recipe was given to my Mom over 45 years ago and we have been using it since, first as a family recipe then when we started baking, this is what we used and have been baking then in our bakery for 25 + years.

Pound Cake:
3 sticks margarine
3 C. flour
3 C. sugar
5 eggs
½ tsp baking powder
1 C. milk
1 tsp vanilla flavoring
1 tsp orange flavoring
1 tsp lemon flavoring

Lemon Glaze:
2 C. powdered sugar
2 tsp lemon flavoring
¼ C. water

Pound Cake:
1. Cream margarine, sugar and eggs; beat till creamy.

2. Add baking powder and flour, alternating with milk.

3. Beat in flavorings until creamy.

4. Bake at 325°F for 1 hour and 20 minutes. Allow to cool.

Lemon Glaze:
1. Lemon glaze really tops this cake off! Mix all ingredients, beat well and spread on cake.

SWARTZENTRUBER'S BAKERY
139 HIGHWAY 28 BYPASS, ABBEVILLE

"When baking, follow directions. When cooking, go by your own taste."
Laiko Bahrs

GRILLED SHRIMP APPETIZER

For a casual and family-friendly environment, head to one of the area's popular TBonz restaurants. Specializing in choice aged beef, fresh local seafood, Lowcountry dishes, grilled salads and Angus Beef burgers. Bring your friends and share a cozy leather booth while enjoying TBonz's acclaimed appetizer, Tommy's Texas cheese fries deluxe. TBonz also features a full service bar including our very own Award-Winning Home-grown Ales. Kids menu and late night menus available. TBonz-Not Just Great Steak!

**(8) 16-20 ct. shrimp, peeled & de-veined
1 oz. liquid margarine
sprinkle lemon pepper seasoning
small amount spring mix
2 oz. Soy-Ginger Sauce (see below)
sprinkle chopped parsley**

**Soy Ginger Sauce (makes 3 qts.)
3 ½ cup of soy sauce
5 C. water
4 C. granulated sugar
½ C. sesame oil
¼ C. roasted garlic
2 Tbsp ginger, freshly minced
1 C. corn starch
8 oz. water**

Grilled Shrimp Appetizer
1. Place the shrimp, on their sides, on the flat top with the liquid margarine. Season with lemon pepper seasoning and cook on both sides. Do not over cook the shrimp.
2. Separately, on a large round plate, mound the spring mix in the center.
3. Line the shrimp, tail side up, around the spring mix and drizzle the soy-ginger sauce over the shrimp and the spring mix.
4. Allow some sauce to create a pool on the plate. Sprinkle chopped parsley on top.

Soy Ginger Sauce
1. In a heavy duty sauce pot, place the soy sauce, 5 cups of water, sesame oil, sugar, garlic and ginger.
2. Bring to a boil, stirring often. Reduce heat by half.
3. Continue to cook for an additional 10 minutes. Remove from heat.
4. Separately, mix together the corn starch and 8 oz. of water to form a thickening paste. Slowly add the paste to the sauce until you reach the desired thickness.
5. Pour the sauce into a plastic container. Label, date, chill and refrigerate.

"I love the culture of grilling. It creates an atmosphere that is festive but casual."
Bobby Flay

Roasted Vegetable Bruschetta

Tee 19 Bar & Bistro at River Falls Plantation

100 Player Boulevard, Duncan

Signature Tastes of SOUTH CAROLINA

Our food group family strives to bring a unique experience of food and service to the Upstate of South Carolina. We're able to base our menus around our Food Group Farm produce, as well as local seasonal products that separate our establishment from other restaurants. We focus on sustainable farming, and the use of local fresh line caught or day boat harvested seafood. We pride ourselves on our practice of "Farm to Table" menu items and an emphasis on providing healthy menu choices.

Pesto:
2 bunches fresh basil
½ C. pecans, toasted
1 oz. fresh garlic
½ C. parmesan cheese
Extra virgin olive oil

Bruschetta:
1 red onion
1 medium carrot
1 medium zucchini
1 medium yellow squash
1 tsp salt
1 tsp pepper
½ Tbsp olive oil
1 loaf French baguette
12 oz. brie cheese
6 oz. balsamic reduction or glaze

Pesto:
1. De-stem basil, then wash and dry. Combine with pecans, garlic and parmesan cheese in food processor.
2. While blending, slowly add olive oil in a stream until all the ingredients are blended together well enough to form a paste. Taste and season as desired.

Bruschetta:
1. Preheat oven to 325°F. Dice the red onion, carrot, zucchini and yellow squash into ¼" cubes. Season with salt, pepper and olive oil.
2. Roast onions and carrots until golden brown. Add in the zucchini and squash and roast for another 5-8 minutes.
3. Cut the baguette into ½" pieces on a bias cut and toast at 325°F for about 3 minutes.
4. Remove from oven and smooth each slice with a small amount of the fresh pesto.
5. Top with a spoonful of the roasted vegetables, followed by a 1 oz. slice of brie cheese.
6. Return to oven just until brie is melted and bruschetta is heated through.
7. Top each slice with a little drizzle of balsamic reduction and enjoy.

Makes 12 servings.

"The greatest delight the fields and woods minister is the suggestion of an occult relation between man and the vegetable.'I am not alone and unacknowledged.' They nod to me and I to them."
Ralph Waldo Emerson (1803-1882)

White Shrimp Remoulade with Fried Green Tomato Salad

We chose the name Terra from the word of Latin origin meaning earth or land. Our goal at Terra is to showcase the beauty and bounty that comes from within. Making a conscious effort to support local farmers and using as many locally grown ingredients as possible, we intend to prepare the freshest and finest ingredients simply so that they speak for themselves. With the addition of a few complementing flavors, we hope to create harmony and beauty with each plate of food. Simple food without pretension.

Signature Taste of SOUTH CAROLINA

2 egg yolks
2 C. canola oil
1 Tbsp Dijon mustard
¼ C. rinsed capers, chopped
2 Tbsp cornichon, minced
1 anchovy filet, chopped
½ tsp paprika
2 dashes Crystal hot sauce
½ lemon, juiced
1 tsp shallot, minced
Spoonful chive & parsley, chopped
Salt to taste
Shrimp, seasoned
Fried Green Tomatoes

1. Whisk egg yolks in a mixing bowl on medium-high speed. Slowly add oil to yolks, pouring a constant stream. It's important to not pour the oil too quickly so the sauce doesn't break. Continue to whip until all oil is incorporated. If too thick, add spoonful of water. Add the capers, cornichon, anchovy and shallots, and stir to combine. Add the lemon juice, hot sauce and herbs, stirring to combine.

2. To make the shrimp, bring court bouillon (water, carrot, onion, celery, bay leaf & lemon) to boil. Add shrimp and cook for a couple of minutes in shell. Pull shrimp when just curled, cool and reserve. Do not cool in ice bath. Peel when cool.

3. At Terra, we fry 2 slices of breaded green tomatoes, seasoned with salt & pepper and cut in half lengthwise. In between the tomato slices, we place 2 strips of Alan Benton's country ham. We toss our salad mix with Dijon mustard vinaigrette (any vinaigrette will suffice). Try not to overdress your salad; the amount of dressing is equally important to the balance between the oil & vinegar. Place lettuce on top of the tomatoes and ham. In a small bowl, place 2 spoonfuls of remoulade, then add 5 shrimp and coat well with sauce. Place shrimp on top of salad and enjoy.

100 STATE STREET, COLUMBIA

TERRA

"There is no sincerer love than the love of food."
George Bernard Shaw

ORANGE & RASPBERRY MARINATED BEETS

Here at Stono Market, we carry the organically grown produce we grow on our Farm as well as a full line of other fruits and veggies year round. We have a country/garden gift shop and the best little lunch café in Charleston, Tomato Shed Café, within our walls. We're quite unique, quaint and friendly. On our farm, Ambrose Family Farm on Wadmalaw Island, we grow strawberries, tomatoes, butter beans, okra, sweet corn, peas, squash, zucchini, onions, collards, potatoes, melons, bedding plants... you get the picture...and we do it naturally and as organically as practical. We field pack our produce to reduce damage from handling and to reduce harvest costs. We deliver the harvest to our Stono Market and local fresh fruit and vegetable venders daily. Our CSA (Community Supported Agriculture) program grows each week. If you want fresh and local, we're the farmer to look to!

6-8 medium fresh, whole beets
1/3 C. shallots, finely chopped
- C. raspberry vinegar
½ C. fresh squeezed orange juice
2 tsp extra virgin olive oil
1 large pinch kosher salt
1 large pinch black pepper
2 navel oranges
2-4 C. baby arugula (may substitute for mixed salad greens)

1. Clean the beets and trim off tops leaving about an inch, so the beets don't bleed out while cooking.

2. Boil beets over high heat approximately 1 to 1 ½ hours or until soft (check with knife if needed).

3. Remove beets from heat, strain and let cool.

4. Using a rag, rub beet peel to remove (you may want to wear gloves).

5. After skins are removed cut beets into cubes.

6. Add shallots, raspberry vinegar, orange juice, extra virgin olive oil, salt & pepper.

7. While marinating, zest one orange and add to mixture.

8. Peel oranges, cut them into chunks and stir together with all other ingredients.

9. Chill for 15-20 minutes then serve over arugula.

Signature Tastes of SOUTH CAROLINA

TOMATO SHED CAFÉ
842 MAIN ROAD, JOHNS ISLAND

"The beet is the most intense of vegetables. The radish, admittedly, is more feverish, but the fire of the radish is a cold fire, the fire of discontent, not of passion. Tomatoes are lusty enough, yet there runs through tomatoes an undercurrent of frivolity. Beets are deadly serious."
Tom Robbins

239

SWEET POTATO CORNBREAD

We've found it quite easy to fill our kitchen and customer's plates with SC's abundant local products. It's our focus in the kitchen to keep the food uncomplicated. Quality is not a foreign concept or product, thus food can be exceptional without being pretentious. Much of the cooking we do is more memory, experience, and a result of the resources in our kitchen, rather than based on a recipe… but we tried to nail this one down for you. Please treat this as more of a suggestion. Tombo Grille Kitchen

3 medium sweet potatoes
6 oz. unsalted butter, cubed, split in ½
½ C. sugar
1/3 C. honey
3 eggs
1 ½ C. whole milk
2 2/3 C. all-purpose flour
1 1/3 C. fine cornmeal
1 ½ Tbsp baking powder
2 oz. rendered bacon fat, split
Salt to taste

1. Wash and place potatoes in a microwave safe dish and cover with plastic. Cook for 5 minutes and follow with 2 minute bursts until fork done.

2. Preheat oven to 350°F.

3. Cream half of the butter with honey and sugar using a stand mixer with a paddle attachment on medium low speed.

4. In a separate bowl, whisk eggs first, then whisk in milk.

5. In a third bowl, sift together the flour, cornmeal, salt and baking powder.

6. On same speed, alternately add the dry and wet ingredients to the butter mixture.

7. Peel and chop the sweet potatoes.

8. Add remaining butter, sweet potatoes and 1oz. bacon fat to mixer and fold ingredients together.

9. Grease a well seasoned cast iron skillet with the remaining 1 oz. bacon fat.

10. Pour contents into greased skillet and bake until a toothpick comes out clean and is golden brown on top.

TOMBO GRILLE
4509 FOREST DRIVE, COLUMBIA

"Happy and successful cooking doesn't rely only on know-how; it comes from the heart, makes great demands on the palate and needs enthusiasm and a deep love of food to bring it to life."
Georges Blanc, 'Ma Cuisine des Saisons'

CRAB CAKES TRAVINIA

Signature Tastes of **SOUTH CAROLINA**

1 lb jumbo lump crab meat
2 eggs
¼ C. green onions, diced
¼ Tbsp Seasons salt
½ oz. lemon juice
¼ Tbsp granulated garlic
- C. dried regular bread crumbs
⅛ C. mayo

1. Mix all ingredients in a bowl except crab meat and breadcrumbs until incorporated.

2. Add crab meat and bread crumbs and fold in by hand being very gentle and careful not to break apart the crab meat.

3. Patty crab cakes into 4 oz. round cakes.

4. Crab cakes can either be baked in an oven at 450°F until golden on the outside, fried at 350°F for about 1 minute or sautéed until there is a golden brown crust on outside.

5. Can be served with a Burre Blanc sauce or just by themselves. Bon appetite!

TRAVINIA ITALIAN KITCHEN
MULTIPLE LOCATIONS ACROSS THE STATE

"So long as you have food in your mouth, you have solved all questions for the time being."
Franz Kafka, Novelist

THE BERGAMO BREAKFAST

At Tristan, fine dining is all about simplicity. We use modern techniques to update classic Italian flavors. We also use modern flavors to accentuate classic Italian cuisine. However, occasionally, we will do something entirely traditional. This is a brunch dish inspired by the cuisine of Bergamo, Italy, where Chef Nate Whiting spent some time.

Signature Tastes of SOUTH CAROLINA

1 C. stone ground polenta
4 C. water
1 oz. extra virgin olive oil
2 oz. butter
A splash of whipping cream
Salt to taste
Frank's Red Hot Sauce to taste
2 oz. Grana Padano, grated
2 oz. Pecorino Romano or Parmigiano Regiano cheese, grated
4 1 oz. pieces of Taleggio cheese, rind removed
8 very fresh large eggs
Clarified butter
Parmesan cheese, grated
Black & red pepper to taste
8 sage leaves, fried till crisp
Chopped chives
Fleur de sel
Freshly ground black pepper
Semi-mild red pepper (we use espelette)
1 oz. whole butter
5 sage leaves, minced
1 Tbsp chopped truffle pieces (optional)
Truffle oil

1. Heat water to a boil. Add the olive oil and a large pinch of salt. Once boiling, swirl in the polenta. Stir constantly until the liquid becomes opaque and yellow. Lower the heat to medium-low, and stir intermittently until the polenta has lost its granular texture (it will still have some texture, but it will not be unpleasant). When the polenta is ready, swirl in 2 oz. butter and a splash of cream. Season to taste with a little more salt, if necessary, and some Frank's hot sauce. Keep hot.

2. In each of 4 bowls with sloping sides, place a piece of Taleggio cheese. If you can't get Taleggio, try to get another funky washed-rind cheese like St. Nectaire or Epoisses, or better yet, Meadow Creek Grayson, which is Virginia's answer to Lombardy's Taleggio. Spoon the hot polenta over the cheese to melt it. Keep these bowls in a warm oven while you cook the eggs.

3. Two eggs at a time, cook the eggs sunny-side up. It's okay to let the heat in your egg pan creep up a little bit. A little frizzle-fry at the edge is a good thing. As each pair of eggs is done, slide them onto the bowls of polenta. Garnish each egg with a little parmesan cheese, chopped chives, fleur de sel and black & red pepper. Top with the fried sage leaves.

4. To finish, heat 1 oz. butter in a pan till it starts to foam and turn brown. Throw in the sage leaves (and the truffle, if you can find it). When it all foams and smells toasty, about a minute, pull it off the heat and drizzle in some truffle oil. Spoon this over the eggs and serve hot.

Serves 4

10 LINGUARD STREET, CHARLESTON
TRISTAN

"Oh, God above, if heaven has a taste it must be an egg with butter and salt, and after the egg is there anything in the world lovelier than fresh warm bread and a mug of sweet golden tea?"
Frank McCourt, 'Angela's Ashes'

BRAISED GROUPER

Victor's Bistro was established in 1989. Since that time, we've become the premier restaurant in Florence. We're the only restaurant in the area serving Certified Angus Beef (CAB), which often arrives from North and South Carolina farms. We pride ourselves on serving only the finest local ingredients available. Our fish and shrimp come from the southeast and our produce from the Pee Dee region. The celebration of good times by good people deserves a place like Victor's.

1 lb fresh grouper
1 bag Carolina Plantation aromatic rice
Chicken stock
10 fresh asparagus stalks
2 vine ripe tomatoes, diced
4 gloves garlic, chopped
1 shallot, diced
½ C. white wine
¼ lb butter, cubed & cold
Salt & fresh ground pepper to taste
2 Tbsp olive oil

1. Cook rice according to package directions, except substitute chicken stock for water and simmer for 20 minutes.

2. Salt & pepper grouper. Add olive oil to hot skillet and gently lay the grouper flat in the pan. The idea is to have the pan hot enough so the grouper doesn't stick to it, but not so hot that it burns.

3. After you've seared one side of the grouper, gently turn it over and reduce the heat.

4. Add garlic, shallot and tomatoes and sauté for 1 minute.

5. Add white wine, butter and asparagus. Cover and reduce heat to low. When the grouper is firm to the touch, it should be done.

6. Gently remove grouper from the skillet, drizzle with sauce from pan and add the asparagus on top. Serve with the rice and enjoy!

"Chef Tommy Crayton brings a unique southern culinary expertise to Victor's Bistro and our diners. Our chef-driven restaurant sets a new standard in Florence dining."
Tim Norwood, Owner

CHICKEN VILLA TRONCO

Family owned and operated for over 70 years. Enjoy casual fine dining in Columbia's oldest and finest Italian restaurant. Located in a historic 19th century Firehouse, we invite you to enjoy our authentic Italian cuisine in an atmosphere of old world charm and southern hospitality.

4 4 oz. boneless chicken breasts
6 oz. artichoke hearts
4 oz. sun-dried tomatoes
8 oz. mushrooms, sliced
2 oz. garlic, chopped
2 C. dry sherry
6 oz. olive oil
5 oz. heavy cream
Salt & pepper to taste

1. Clean chicken of fat and/or bones (if buying split breasts).

2. Flour chicken and sauté in olive oil until golden brown.

3. Add artichoke hearts, sun-dried tomatoes, mushrooms, garlic and salt & pepper. Sauté with the chicken until cooked.

4. Add sherry and burn off alcohol.

5. Add heavy cream and reduce sauce by one-third. Serve with favorite starch and wine.

Serves 4

VILLA TRONCO

1213 BLANDING STREET, COLUMBIA

"The trouble with eating Italian food is that 5 or 6 days later you're hungry again."
George Miller, British writer

FRUIT GALETTE

Welcome to The Village Baker! We feature artisan breads, pastries, cookies, bagels and pizza all made from scratch. We are located in historic downtown Pendleton on the square across from the Farmers Hall. We're family owned and operated and enjoy getting to know our customers and introducing them to the best baked goods money can buy.

Crust:
1 1/3 C. all-purpose flour
1 tsp salt
8 oz. unsalted butter, chilled & cut into cubes
3-4 Tbsp ice water
Eggs, for wash

Peach & Almond Filling:
1 lb free stone peaches
¼ C. peach jam (or apricot)
2 Tbsp tapioca flour (or cornstarch)
1 Tbsp lemon juice
¼ C. coarse sugar (turbinado)
4 oz. almond paste
1-2 Tbsp warm water

Crust:
1. Blend salt and flour together. Cut cubed butter into flour with knife or pie cutter. When mixture is crumbly (pea size), add cold water and mix until dough starts to form.
2. Place dough onto a square of wax paper or food film, press together. Shape dough like a log, wrap with film, then refrigerate for 30-45 minutes while making the filling.
3. After dough has rested, take log and cut into 3 even pieces. Roll out 1 piece at a time on a floured wooden or marble surface to approximately ¼" thickness into a round shape. Don't worry about the edges being uneven. Set aside and repeat procedure with the remaining 2 pieces.
4. Place all 3 rounds on a parchment lined pan (or use silpat). Place a 1/3 of the almond paste in the center of each round and spread it out, keeping at least 1" from edge.
5. Place 1/3 of the peach filling on top of almond paste. Moisten outside edges of rounds with water and start folding 2" of dough toward middle (fold 1" up) over the peach filling. The crust should be pleated with each fold.
6. Once the crust has been completely pleated around the filling, wash the crust with egg wash and sprinkle with turbinado sugar. Bake in a preheated 375°F oven for approximately 30-40 minutes or until crust is brown and filling starts to bubble.

Peach & Almond Filling:
1. Peel the peaches and cut into slices. Drizzle with lemon juice. Blend jam with tapioca starch and add to peaches. Soften almond paste with warm water.

You can substitute apples, pears, plums, or cherries for the peaches (for cherries or plums double the corn starch used).

Signature Tastes of SOUTH CAROLINA

THE VILLAGE BAKER
108 E. MAIN STREET, PENDLETON

"A fruit is a vegetable with looks and money. Plus, if you let fruit rot, it turns into wine, something Brussels sprouts never do."
P. J. O'Rourke

GOAT CHEESE BRUSCHETTA

Signature Tastes of SOUTH CAROLINA

VIRTU RESTAURANT & BAR
2406 DEVINE STREET, COLUMBIA

Roasted Tomato Vinaigrette:
- 1 small shallot
- 1 Tbsp Dijon or Creole mustard
- 1 Tbsp honey
- 2 medium sized roasted tomatoes
- - C. red wine vinegar
- 1 ¼ C. olive oil + 2 Tbsp
- Kosher salt & fresh ground pepper to taste

Goat Cheese Bruschetta:
- 6 medium/large vine ripe tomatoes
- 6 cloves garlic, roasted
- 12-15 basil leaves
- ¾ C. Roasted Tomato Vinaigrette
- 4 oz. goat cheese crumbles (Chevre)
- 1 baguette
- Olive oil for brushing
- Salt & pepper to taste

Balsamic Reduction:
- 1 ¼ C. balsamic vinegar
- ¼ C. sugar

Goat Cheese Bruschetta:

1. Chop tomatoes into a medium dice. Roughly chop basil leaves and finely mince garlic. Place all ingredients into a large bowl and mix thoroughly. Season with salt & pepper. Cover and store in refrigerator overnight.
2. Preheat oven to 325°F. Cut baguette diagonally into ¾" slices. Brush with olive oil and season with salt & pepper. Bake for 7-8 minutes or until crispy. Allow crustinies to cool at room temperature.

Balsamic Reduction:

1. Place both ingredients in small saucepan and reduce by about half over low heat, stirring occasionally. Mixture should coat a spoon but still be slightly runny when finished. Allow to cool at room temperature.

Roasted Tomato Vinaigrette:

1. Preheat oven to 350°F. Cut each tomato into four wedges and squeeze out the seeds. Toss the wedges with 2 Tbsp olive oil and season with salt & pepper. Place in a metal 9" cake pan and roast in oven for 20-30 minutes or until skins begin to blister and tomatoes are soft. Remove from oven and allow to cool.
2. Place shallot, mustard, honey, tomatoes and vinegar in a food processor and puree. With food processor running, slowly drizzle in olive oil. Season with salt & pepper.

To serve: Place crustinies on large plate and, using a slotted spoon, scoop bruschetta mixture on top of each one. Crumble goat cheese over the top of the bruschetta and garnish with a drizzle of the balsamic reduction.

"Age is not important unless you're a cheese."
Helen Hayes

253

BANANA SPLIT PIE

Signature Tastes of SOUTH CAROLINA

1 C. powdered sugar
½ C. butter, room temp
¼ C. liquid eggs
½ tsp vanilla extract
1 graham cracker
pie crust
2 bananas, sliced
20 oz. can crushed
pineapple, well drained
2 C. whipped topping
Chopped pecans
Chocolate sauce
Maraschino cherry

1. Beat first 4 ingredients at medium speed with an electric mixer until fluffy and smooth.

2. Spread the mixture into the bottom of the graham cracker pie shell.

3. Top filling with sliced bananas, followed by drained pineapple.

4. Finish with whipped topping, sealing the edges.

5. Sprinkle with chopped pecans. Chill for 1 hour.

6. Garnish before serving with chocolate sauce and top with a maraschino cherry.

WADES FAMILY RESTAURANT
1000 N. PINE STREET, SPARTANBURG

"Never interrupt me when I'm eating a banana."
Ryan Stiles, Actor

CORNBREAD DRESSING

SOUTH CAROLINA

Signature Tastes of

If you live anywhere in or around the Pee Dee, you most likely have eaten at or at least heard of Webster Manor. For 25 years, Webster Manor has been more than just the "local's favorite" – people drive from all over to enjoy our weekday lunch of Southern cuisine, buffet-style. While every day is a wonderful day at Webster Manor, Thursdays are a particular favorite as Turkey and Dressing are on the buffet. Rumored as the best around, dressing is bought by the pan during the holidays by those wishing to serve up "Webster's dressing" instead of their own.

**10 boiled eggs
1 celery stalk
1 large onion
Turkey stock (enough to create a moist consistency)
Corn muffins & bread rolls (~ 4 qt.)
¼ C. hot sauce
Salt & pepper to taste**

1. Finely chop the eggs, celery and onion in a food processor.

2. Add the egg and vegetable mixture to the corn muffins and bread rolls.

3. Pour in the turkey stock and the hot sauce and mix to a consistency you like.

4. Bake at 375°F for about 1 hour.

WEBSTER MANOR
115 E. JAMES STREET, MULLINS

"The North thinks it knows how to make corn bread, but this is a gross superstition. Perhaps no bread in the world is quite as good as Southern corn bread, and perhaps no bread in the world is quite as bad as the Northern imitation of it."
Mark Twain

TACOS CAROLINA

Windy Hill Orchard is a family owned and operated boutique apple orchard and cider mill. Open every Fall from mid-August until Christmas, we offer visitors, Pick Your Own Apples, Fresh Pressed Apple Cider, Farm Tours, Fresh Made Apple Products, and much, much more.

4 4 oz. boneless, skinless chicken breasts
10 Tbsp Windy Hill Orchard Apple Butter BBQ Sauce
2/3 C. red cabbage, shredded
2/3 C. carrots, grated
2/3 C. broccoli stem, shredded
10 Tbsp honey Dijon salad dressing
4 whole wheat tortillas

1. Brush the chicken breasts with BBQ sauce and grill until tender.

2. While the chicken is grilling, toss shredded cabbage, carrots and broccoli with honey Dijon dressing to make coleslaw.

3. When the chicken comes off the grill, cut it up into bite-sized pieces.

4. Wrap the chicken and coleslaw in the whole wheat tortillas, and you've got great tasting, healthy, Tacos Carolina!

Serves 4

WINDY HILL ORCHARD & CIDER MILL
1860 BLACK HIGHWAY, YORK

"One taste of a hot apple cider doughnut and you will understand the quest that led to this business. Those in the know start coming the first week of September for the hot, fresh doughnuts."
Jayne Scarborough, You Don't Get Apple Cider From a Cow

SKILLET-FRIED SC QUAIL WITH DIRTY RICE & GRILLED SCALLIONS

Unique to the island for its casual yet sophisticated urban feel, WiseGuys has fast become a local see-and-be-seen hot spot. Featuring an award winning Big Wines list of over 150 bottles, with over 50 by the glass. The Small Plates menu at WiseGuys takes cocktail party dining to a new level with fresh local farm to table ingredients as well as incredible international flavors, globally inspired cuisine, and fun and exciting presentations that will exceed your every expectation. The cutting edge Serious Cocktail list lights up the nightlife with unique and original libations that change with the seasons. WiseGuys invites you through the stainless steel doors, into the plush and friendly environment to sample the wines, savor the food, and share our passion!

Fried Quail:
4 Semi-boneless quail, split in half from top to bottom
¼ C. flour
1 tsp salt
⅛ tsp pepper

Dirty Rice:
1 ½ C. Carolina Plantation rice
2 C. chicken stock
2 C. water
3 Tbsp olive oil
½ lb ground pork
½ C. chicken livers
3 slices bacon, chopped
½ onion, chopped
2 celery stalks, chopped
½ green bell pepper or 1-3 jalapenos, seeded & chopped
1 Tbsp Cajun seasoning

Grilled Scallions:
12 Medium sized scallions
Olive oil
Coarse sea salt or Kosher salt
Cracked pepper

Fried Quail:
1. Dredge quail with mixture of flour, salt & and pepper. Have cast iron skillet half filled with hot oil. Brown quail on both sides. Reduce heat. Cook slowly until tender, about 20 minutes, turning once to brown evenly.

Dirty Rice:
1. Cook the rice according to the package instructions, but use chicken stock for - of the cooking liquid. Once the rice has finished cooking, remove from heat and let sit for 5 minutes. Turn the rice out onto a sheet pan and drizzle 1 tablespoon of olive oil over it. Mix to combine and let cool.
2. While the rice is cooking, mash and finely chop the chicken livers or purée briefly in a blender. In a large pan that can eventually hold the rice plus everything else, put 1 Tbsp of oil plus the bacon and cook over medium-low heat until the bacon is crispy.
3. Add the ground pork and increase the heat to high. Allow the meat to brown before stirring. As soon as the pork starts to brown, add the final Tbsp of oil, celery, jalapenos and onions. Brown over medium-high heat. You may notice the bottom of the pan getting crusty. Keep it from burning by lowering the heat if needed. Add the minced liver and cook for a few minutes more.
4. Add the remaining cup of chicken stock and deglaze the pan by scraping the bottom of the pan with a wooden spoon. Add the Cajun seasoning and turn the heat to high. Boil away most of the chicken stock and then add the cooked rice. Toss to combine. Turn off the heat. Serve hot.

Grilled Scallions:
1. Trim the root end from the scallions and discard. Sprinkle the scallions with just enough olive oil to coat. Season liberally with salt & pepper. Grill briefly on a very hot grill until slightly charred and limp. Remove from the grill and keep warm.

To serve: Divide the dirty rice onto four plates. Place two quail halves on each portion of the rice. Top the quail with three of the grilled scallions. Enjoy.

1513 MAIN STREET, HILTON HEAD ISLAND

WISEGUYS

"Rice is the best, the most nutritive and unquestionably the most wide-spread staple in the world."
Escoffier

Italian Orzo with Collard Greens & Fresh Collard Dip

Signature Taste of SOUTH CAROLINA

The Rawl family history is a story of love, faith and perseverance. In 1925, Walter Rawl and Ernestine Price were married and shortly after, they borrowed some money from his father to purchase 48 acres of land. Farming had been in his family for years but his dad still told him he would never make enough off that land to pay back the loan. Walter and Ernestine both worked hard on the land and had the motto "Sell what you can, Can what you can't." Working in a variety of areas from canning, chickens, peaches, sweet potatoes, and eventually collards, they were able to gain valuable respect in the industry. They loved their God, family, community, and their land. It wouldn't be long until they were known as the Collard King and Queen. Now resting on the shoulders of the 3rd generation, they have become Walter P. Rawl & Sons, Inc. a major grower, processor and shipper of quality fresh vegetables available in stores nationwide. None of us will ever know if it was his love of the land or the fatherly "motivation" he received that has made WP Rawl so successful, but we do know they will stay true to the motto they were raised on "Take care of the land and it will take care of you."

Italian Orzo with Collard Greens:
1 C. uncooked orzo
1 tsp salt
2 tsp dried Italian herbs
4 Tbsp olive oil, divided
2 cloves garlic, minced
1 C. grape tomatoes, sliced in half
1 (1-lb size) NATURE'S GREENS™ Bagged Collards
1 large lemon, juiced
¼ C. parmesan cheese, grated
Salt & pepper to taste

Fresh Collard Dip:
1 (1 lb size) NATURE'S GREENS™ Bagged Collards
1 (1.4-oz size) pkg. Dry Vegetable Soup/Dip Recipe Mix
1 16 oz. container sour cream
1 C. mayo
1 (5-oz. size) RAWL BRAND VERSATILE VEGGIES™ Diced Green Onions
2 dashes Worcestershire sauce

Italian Orzo with Collard Greens:
1. Bring large pot of salted water to a boil. Add orzo and return to boil. Cook uncovered, stirring occasionally until pasta has cooked through about 6-9 minutes. Drain. Return to pot; add Italian herbs and toss. Cover and set aside.
2. In a large stock pot, add 2 Tbsp olive oil on medium heat. Add garlic, tomatoes and sauté for 2-3 minutes. Remove garlic and tomatoes and set aside.
3. Add remaining olive oil to same stock pot on medium heat. Add collard greens, toss to coat and sauté for 10 minutes, stirring occasionally. Add orzo, garlic, tomatoes, and lemon juice. Stir and continue cooking for 5 minutes.
4. Stir in parmesan cheese and season with salt & pepper. Serve warm or at room temperature. Serves 6-8.

Fresh Collard Dip:
1. Finely chop collards and cook in a small amount of water for 10 minutes. Strain and pat dry 2-3 cups of the cooked collards.
2. In a medium bowl, combine collards with remaining ingredients. Cover and chill at least 2 hours to blend flavors. Serve with corn scoops or crackers.

WP RAWL & SONS, INC.
824 FAIRVIEW ROAD, PELION

"Love, like a chicken salad or restaurant hash, must be taken with blind faith or it loses its flavor."
Helen Rowland

263

Yoder's
DUTCH
KITCHEN
Abbeville, S.C.
"Specializing in Penna.
Dutch Cooking"

Broccoli & Rice Casserole

This restaurant specializes in fresh garden ingredients from local Mennonite farms. This restaurant is more than the traditional meat and three. It is a vegetarian delight. Desserts are made fresh daily. You never walk away hungry. It is open Wednesday through Saturday. Sometimes there will be a line to get in.

1 qt. chopped broccoli (or 1 lb. fresh)
1 pt. cooked rice
1 C. onions, chopped
1 C. celery, chopped
½ stick butter
1 pt. Cheez Whiz
2 cans cream of mushroom soup
Bread crumbs
Dash of salt & white pepper

1. Cook broccoli until slightly soft, then drain well.

2. Cook the celery, onions and butter together until soft.

3. Add Cheez Whiz and soup and cook until cheese melts.

4. Add to broccoli, rice and then season with salt & pepper.

5. Bake in shallow pan for 20 minutes at 350°F. For best results, cover with tin foil.

6. After 20 minutes, remove tin foil and cover casserole with bread crumbs. Return to oven and bake until cheese melts.

Signature Tastes of SOUTH CAROLINA

YODER'S DUTCH KITCHEN
809 E. GREENWOOD STREET, ABBEVILLE

"Newman, you wouldn't eat broccoli if it was deep-fried in chocolate sauce."
Jerry Seinfeld to Newman in 'The Chicken Roaster'
episode of 'Seinfeld' TV series.

INDEX O' RECIPES

"I should have no objection to go over the same life from its beginning to the end: requesting only the advantage authors have, of correcting in a second edition the faults of the first."
Benjamin Franklin

Steven W. Siler is a firefighter-cum-chef serving in Bellingham, Washington. Long marinated in the epicurean heritage of the Deep South, Steven has spent over 20 years (dear God has it been that long?!) in the much-vaulted restaurant industry from BOH to FOH to chef. In addition, he has served as an editor and contributing writer for several food publications. When not trying to shove food down his fellow firefighters' gullets, he enjoys sailing and sampling the finest of scotches and wines, and has an irrational love affair with opera. He swears one day he will relive the above picture on the Gulf Coast with a good Will.

The Signature Tastes series of cookbooks is the one of the first of a series of culinary celebrations from Smoke Alarm Media, based in the Pacific Northwest. Smoke Alarm Media is named for another series of unfortunate culinary accidents at an unnamed fire department, also in the Pacific Northwest. One of the founders was an active firefighter. Having been trained as a chef, he found himself in the position of cooking frequently at the fire station. Alas, his culinary skills were somewhat lacking in using the broiler and smoke would soon fill the kitchen and station. The incidents became so frequent that the 911 dispatch would call the station and ask if "Chef Smoke Alarm" would kindly refrain from cooking on his shift. Thus Smoke Alarm Media was born.

 SIGNATURE TASTES   **HIDDEN EATS**   **TABLE FACTS**   **BYGONE ERAS**   **ART OF CULINARY DIPLOMACY**   **VARSITY**    **SUBLIME NECTAR**